NEW VISTAS

3

WORKBOOK

H. DOUGLAS BROWN

ANNE ALBARELLI-SIEGFRIED

ALICE SAVAGE • MASOUD SHAFIEI

Longman

New Vistas 3 Workbook

Pearson Education, 10 Bank Street, White Plains, NY 10606

Editorial director: Allen Ascher
Project manager: Margaret Grant
Development editor: Lorna Joy Swain
Director of design and production: Rhea Banker
Associate director of design and development: Aliza Greenblatt
Executive managing editor: Linda Moser
Production manager: Ray Keating
Production editor: Martin Yu
Digital layout specialist: Rachel Baumann
Director of manufacturing: Patrice Fraccio
Senior manufacturing buyer: Edith Pullman
Photo research: Patricia Lattanzio
Cover design: Carmine Vecchio
Text design: Eric Dawson
Illustrators: Andrew Lange, Don Martinetti, Catherine Sullivan, Carlotta Tormey
Realia:Rachel Baumann
Photo credits: p. 26, Helen Keller, Library of Congress; p. 26, Dr. Chien-Shiung Wu, © Bettmann/CORBIS.

Reviewers

Robert A. Cote, *Lindsey Hopkins Technical Education Center*; Ulysses D'Aquila, *City College of San Francisco*; M. Sadiq Durrani, *BNC Santa Cruz*; Charles M. García, *University of Texas–Brownsville*; Kathleen Huggard Gómez, *Hunter College*; Kathy Hamilton, *Elk Grove Adult Education*; Kevin Keating, *University of Arizona*; Rosa Moreno, *Instituto Cultural Peruano–Norteamericano*; Betty Otiniano, *Instituto Cultural Peruano–Norteamericano*; Herbert D. Pierson, *St. John's University*; Alison M. Rice, *Hunter College*; Maria Rita Vieira, *Yazigi Language School*; Tammy Smith-Firestone, *Edgewood Language Institute*; Garnet Templin-Imel, *Bellevue Community College*

ISBN 0-13-908286-7

2 3 4 5 6 7 8 9 10—BAH—05 04 03 02 01 00

Contents

Dear Student,

This workbook gives you many interesting exercises to help you to improve your English. The exercises will give you a chance to practice the English that you learned in the classroom. They also can be used to test yourself on how much you have learned in your class lessons. You can use the workbook at home by yourself, or in class with a classmate. If any of the exercises or items are too difficult for you, ask a classmate for help, or if your teacher has time, ask your teacher. You might also look at the Grammar Summary Page in your *Student Book*.

Enjoy using this workbook!

H. Douglas Brown

Professor of English
Director of the American
    Language Institute
San Francisco State University
San Francisco, California

UNIT 1

Lesson 1 He was born in Venezuela.

Exercise 1

Look at the timeline tracing the history of Miguel Hernandez, a successful doctor in San Antonio, Texas.

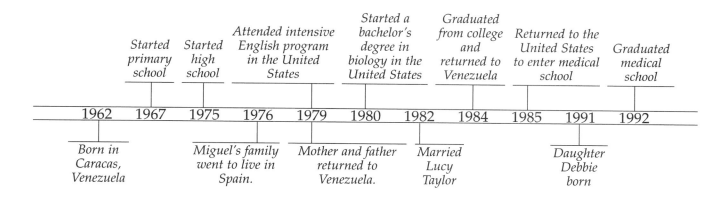

Read each sentence and circle *T* (true) or *F* (false). Then on the lines below, rewrite the false sentences, making them true.

1. Miguel started primary school while his family still lived in Caracas.   T   F
2. Miguel's mother took him to Spain while he was in high school.   T   F
3. Miguel moved back to Venezuela while he was in college.   T   F
4. Miguel's parents returned to Venezuela while Miguel was studying English in the United States.   T   F
5. Miguel got married while he was working on his bachelor's degree.   T   F
6. Miguel's daughter was born while he was attending medical school.   T   F

_____

_____

_____

_____

_____

Complete the paragraph that Miguel's daughter, Debbie, wrote about her parents.

My mother met my father while she (*attend*) _____ college at the University of
Texas in Austin. They (*walk*) _____ toward each other in the cafeteria in the middle of
a big storm, and suddenly the lights went out. It was dark and my mother (*walk*) _____
right into my father's arms. At least that is what he said. While they (*wait*) _____ for
the electricity to come back on, they (*start*) _____ talking, and pretty soon they fell in
love. My mother (*want, not*) _____ to get married while she (*take*) _____
classes, so they waited until she (*have*) _____ her degree. My father says that it was
hard for him to wait, but he did, and now they are very happy.

Answer the following questions about your past on the lines below. Then, on a separate sheet
of paper, make a timeline with important events from your own life. Use your responses to the
questions as a guide.

1. Where did you live when you were growing up?
2. What year did you start school?
3. Did anything interesting happen while you were going to school?
4. Did anything interesting happen while you were living in a particular place?
5. Did any other important events take place while you were growing up?

1. _____
2. _____
3. _____
4. _____
5. _____

Exercise 4

Choose one event from your timeline—a graduation, a new boyfriend or girlfriend, or a new baby, for example—and describe the experience in a paragraph. Use the following questions as a guide.

1. When did the event take place?
2. Where were you when it happened? What did the place look like?
3. Who were you with?
4. What happened? Give as many details as you can.
5. How did you feel about it?

_____

_____

_____

_____

_____

_____

Exercise 5

Look at the expressions for ending a conversation on page 4 of your Student Book and write a dialog for each situation on the lines below.

1. _____

_____

2. _____

_____

3. _____

_____

4. _____

_____

Lesson 2   I'm going to work harder.

=========== **Exercise 1** ===========

Look at the following pictures. For each situation, write a sentence with *hope* and the phrase in parentheses.

(become a teacher)

1. <u>Linda hopes she'll become a</u>
   <u>teacher in the future.</u>

(buy a house)

2. _____

_____

(get better)

3. _____

_____

(be famous)

4. _____

_____

(find a job)

5. _____

_____

(not fail the test)

6. _____

_____

The following language-learning strategies can help you improve your English more quickly. Write a sentence with *be going to* or *will* for each item. Then add one more strategy that you plan to use during the semester.

1. use a monolingual dictionary

   _____

2. read novels and magazines in English

   _____

3. keep a daily journal in English

   _____

4. speak more in class

   _____

5. find a pen pal

   _____

6. make a list of new words

   _____

7. do all my assignments

   _____

8. _____

Some language-learning strategies are more helpful than others. Answer the following questions about your learning-strategy plans for this semester. Then number the strategies according to their importance to you.

_____ Are you going to watch movies in English to improve your listening comprehension?

   Yes, I am. I'm going to rent videos and watch them at home.

_____ Are you going to speak English to classmates who are from your country?

   _____

_____ Are you going to write the meaning of new words in your native language?

   _____

_____ Are you going to be quiet in class?

   _____

_____ Are you going to try to memorize all the grammar rules?

   _____

Mr. and Mrs. Robinson are going to work in Turkey for the next three years. Use *must, have to,* or *don't have to* and the following phrases to indicate what the Robinsons do and do not have to do before they leave. Include additional information to make your sentences more interesting.

1. obtain passports — They have to obtain passports to leave the country.

2. close their bank accounts — They don't have to close their bank accounts in the United States.

3. ship their furniture — _____

4. learn Turkish — _____

5. buy plane tickets — _____

6. rent a house in Turkey — _____

7. learn about the new culture — _____

8. sell their house — _____

Exercise 5

Make predictions about your future (ten years from now) by answering the following questions.

1. How old will you be?

_____

2. What kind of job will you have?

_____

3. Will you be married?

_____

4. Will you have children? How many?

_____

5. Where will you live?

_____

6. What will you do during your free time?

_____

Lesson 3 Kevin likes horror movies.

Exercise 1

Complete the story with verbs in the present or past tense.

Lisa's daily activities seldom vary. She usually _____1_____ at 7:00 A.M. Then she _____2_____ a bath and _____3_____ breakfast. She always _____4_____ the newspaper before she _____5_____ for school. She often _____6_____ to school because she _____7_____ only a few blocks away. She _____8_____ classes in the mornings and _____9_____ in the library in the afternoons.

Yesterday was a little different. Lisa _____10_____ her breakfast as usual. But when she was ready to leave for school, the phone _____11_____. A friend _____12_____ to invite her to a party on Saturday night. They _____13_____ for over half an hour, so Lisa _____14_____ her first class. When she _____15_____ at school, she _____16_____ to the library to work on her term paper. But the library was closed. Lisa then _____17_____ at the school calendar only to discover that it was Saturday!

Exercise 2

Read the strategies for learning English in the chart. Martin checked the strategies he uses and made an ✗ next to the strategies he doesn't use. Look at Martin's checklist and write sentences describing his study habits.

1. Make clear, concise notes when you are listening to a class discussion or a lecture.	✓
2. Learn correct pronunciation by looking up the phonetic symbols in the dictionary.	✗
3. Write the words you want to remember in a notebook and then look at them whenever you have a spare moment.	✗
4. Take an active role in class. Ask questions, take risks, and be prepared to try new things.	✓
5. Organize your vocabulary lists by topic.	✓
6. Don't translate everything into your native language.	✓

1. Martin makes clear, concise notes when he is listening to a class discussion or a lecture.
2. _____
3. _____
4. _____
5. _____
6. _____

Look at Kevin's questionnaire and write sentences with *and . . . too* or *and . . . not either.*

COMPUTER DATA SERVICE

Check your likes and dislikes.

Name   Kevin Stoka

	LIKE	DON'T LIKE			LIKE	DON'T LIKE
1. Movies				**2. Sports**		
Musical Comedies		✔		Soccer	✔	
Horror	✔			Baseball		✔
Science Fiction	✔			Tennis		✔
Westerns		✔		Swimming	✔	
3. TV Programs				**4. Music**		
News		✔		Classical		✔
Documentaries	✔			Jazz	✔	
Game Shows	✔			Country		✔
Talk Shows		✔		Rock	✔	

1. Kevin likes horror movies, and he likes science fiction movies too.
2. Kevin doesn't like musical comedies, and he doesn't like Westerns either.
3. _____
4. _____
5. _____
6. _____
7. _____
8. _____

Write two sentences about the type of entertainment you like or dislike.

9. _____
10. _____

Complete the following sentences using *and . . . too, and . . . not either,* or *but.*

Golden Palace MENU

Cantonese Chicken
Peking Duck
Sweet and Sour Spare Ribs
Ribs
Egg Rolls
Beef with Snow Peas
Shrimp and Chow Mein

The Gondola

Menu

Chicken Florentine
Cheese Ravoli
Minestrone Soup
Veal Scaloppini
Beef Lasagna
Shrimp Alfredo

Buena Vista MENU

Chicken Fajitas
Beef Fajitas
Taco Salad
Barbecued Spare Ribs
Tortilla Soup
Chili con Carne

1. The Golden Palace serves chicken, <u>and the Gondola and Buena Vista do too.</u>
    (the Gondola/Buena Vista)

2. The Gondola doesn't serve duck, <u>but the Golden Palace does.</u>
    (the Golden Palace)

3. The Golden Palace doesn't serve veal, _____
    (Buena Vista)

4. Buena Vista doesn't serve shrimp, _____
    (the Golden Palace/the Gondola)

5. The Gondola serves soup, _____
    (Buena Vista)

6. The Golden Palace serves egg rolls, _____
    (the Gondola)

7. Buena Vista serves beef, _____
    (the Golden Palace/the Gondola)

8. The Golden Palace doesn't serve chili con carne, _____
    (Buena Vista)

9. The Gondola serves lasagna, _____
    (the Golden Palace/Buena Vista)

10. The Golden Palace doesn't serve chili, _____
    (the Gondola)

UNIT 2

Lesson 1 I've been to Brazil.

Exercise 1

Look at the map and write a statement in the speech balloon for each person. Then answer the questions.

1. Who has traveled to the coldest climate? _____

2. Who has traveled to the smallest country? _____

3. Who has traveled to the largest country? _____

Sheda is doing a geography project on earthquakes. Read her notes and make them into complete sentences.

Japan: Many earthquakes, central area. Tokyo 1923, Kobe 1995.

Iran: Many earthquakes, northeastern mountains. Severe quakes, strikes in recent history, 1978, 1990, 1997

United States: West Coast. California: major quakes in 1971, 1989.

Iran has experienced several earthquakes in the northeastern mountains. The worst quakes in recent history occurred in 1978, 1990, and 1997.

Complete this paragraph from Sheda's earthquake report. Use the appropriate form of the verbs given.

Earthquakes (*cause*) _____ a great deal of destruction ever since people can

remember. As a result, humans (*search*) _____ for ways to create safer conditions in

cities built on fault lines. Their success in saving property and lives has been varied. Hard-hitting

quakes in Kobe, Japan, in 1995 and in northern Iran in 1990 and 1997 (*destroy*) _____

older buildings and homes and caused tens of thousands of deaths. However, architects and

scientists (*manage*) _____ to lessen the danger in new construction for the last couple

of decades. Many of the newer buildings sway with the motion of the quake rather than collapse.

Modern cities such as Tokyo and San Francisco (*lower*) _____ the number

earthquake-related deaths as a result.

Has your area experienced an earthquake, volcanic eruption, or other natural disaster? Answer the questions with complete sentences. Use correct tenses.

1. What natural event or events have happened in your area?

   _____

2. When did the most recent event happen?

   _____

3. How much time has passed since the most recent event?

   _____

4. Do you think it will happen again?

   _____

Proofread a draft of a paragraph about snowstorms and blizzards in the United States. Find and correct seven mistakes. There is one error in each of the numbered sentences. (Hint: Look at the meaning as well as the tense of each verb.)

                             lived
(1) People who have ~~live~~ in snow country know about blizzards and whiteouts. (2) They are heavy snowstorms with high winds, and they were responsible for numerous deaths in northern states since the time of the early settlers. (3) People who have experiencing them tell stories of feeling totally lost or of losing loved ones. (4) One man has walked from his house to his garage when the storm came. (5) When he has not come back, his wife went out to look for him. Rescuers found their bodies miles away. However, tragedies like this one can be avoided.

(6) Many residents of northern climates have tying a rope between their garage and the house.

(7) When they get caught by a storm, they have use the rope to guide themselves to safety.

Lesson 2   You shouldn't eat in class.

Complete the students' and Mr. Robinson's conversations with appropriate expressions.

1. **Jacques:** Hi, my name is Jacques.
   Tony: Hello, Jacques. <u>My name is Tony.</u>
   Jacques: Nice to meet you, Tony.
   Tony: <u>Nice to meet you, too.</u>

2. **Lynn:** Mom, Dad, this is Gina, my classmate. Gina, my parents.
   Mr. Wang: _____?
   Gina: I'm fine, thanks. How do you do?
   Mrs. Wang: _____.

Mr. Robinson

3. **Sofia:** Mr. Robinson?
   Mr. Robinson: Yes.
   Sofia: Hello. _____.
   Mr. Robinson: Hello, Sofia. _____
   _____?
   Sofia: I'm fine, thanks. How are you?
   Mr. Robinson: _____.

4. **Nelson:** Jacques, it's a wonderful party, but I've got to go. It was great to finally meet you.
   Jacques: _____.

Complete the conversations with *may, can, may not,* or *can't* to indicate permission; *can* or *can't* to indicate ability; and *may* or *may not* to indicate possibility.

1. **Tony:** _____ I borrow your pen?

   Yumiko: Sure. Actually, you _____ keep it. I have two more.

2. **Mr. Robinson:** Nelson looks very athletic.

   Oscar: Yes, he _____ run for two hours without stopping.

3. **Lynn:** _____ you open the door for me? My hands are full.

   Ivan: Sure.

4. **Oscar:** This box is so heavy I _____ even lift it.

   Nelson: Let me see if I _____ do it.

5. **Lynn:** _____ we drink sodas in the computer lab, Mr. Robinson?

   Mr. Robinson: No, you _____ . You _____ drink them outside, though.

6. **Nelson:** _____ you tell me where Mr. Robinson is?

   Secretary: I'm not sure where he is. He _____ be in his office.

7. **Gina:** Are you going to the beach with us tomorrow?

   Yumiko: No, I don't think so. It _____ rain tomorrow, and I don't want to be outside if it does.

8. **Jacques:** _____ I use the computers in the lab to send personal e-mail?

   Mr. Robinson: No, you _____ . These computers are not linked to the Internet.

Make a request or offer using *may* or *can* for each of the situations.

1. You're in a restaurant eating a hamburger. You notice that there's no ketchup on your table, but there are two bottles of ketchup on the table next to you. What would you say to ask for ketchup?

   _____

2. You call your friend, but her roommate tells you she isn't home. You want to leave a message for your friend. What would you say to the roommate?

   _____

3. You work in a bookstore, and you notice that a customer is looking around for help. What would you say to the customer?

   _____

4. You want to make a phone call but have no coins. How would you ask someone for change?

   _____

5. You have to leave class early. How would you ask your teacher to let you leave early?

   _____

Look at the following pictures. Write a question with *should* for each picture. Then write the answers to the questions.

(study in front of the TV)

1. Should she study in front of the TV?
   No, she shouldn't.

(wear a cap in class)

2. _____

(we / translate every new word)

3. _____

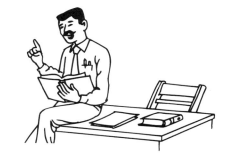

(sit on the table)

4. _____

(wear uniforms to school)

5. _____

(put makeup on in class)

6. _____

Look at the composition Robin wrote about her ideal English class. Then answer the questions.

My Ideal English Class
By Robin Lee

The ideal English class should have special characteristics. First of all, our teacher ought to let us eat whenever we want. Hamburgers, hot dogs, pizza, soda, gum, and ice cream should be allowed in class at any time.

Next, everyone should get good grades for the effort they put into the work. The teacher should grade like Mr. Robinson because he grades based on class participation, unlike Mrs. Burnett, who gives hours of homework. We ought to be able to do the assignments in class, not at home.

Finally, we should be able to have fun in our classroom. A classroom shouldn't be a boring place to learn. People ought to have fun in their lives every day. Dancing and listening to music, therefore, should be part of the class.

1. Which sentence states the main idea of the composition? _____

_____

2. What three sentences support the main idea? _____

_____

_____

Write a short essay in your notebook about the characteristics your ideal English class or school should have. Use Robin's composition as an example. When you finish, check your essay.

- Does your essay have a title?
- Is there a margin at each side of the paper?
- Did you indent each paragraph?
- Does your essay have a main idea?
- Does your essay have supporting sentences?
- Did you proofread for spelling, punctuation, capitalization, and grammar?

Lesson 3   I know I'm not alone.

Read the following university students' comments about living in a new culture. Then complete the sentences that follow.

"Living in the United States has helped me appreciate the good things in both the Chinese and American cultures. Which culture I belong to is not an issue anymore. What is important to me now is the kind of person I want to be. I am happy that I haven't found any essential conflict between the two cultures."

—*Wei Li, People's Republic of China (Chemistry)*

"My most difficult time was the first term here. I had to get up at 6:00 in the morning, and I went to class in the dark. When I came back, it was dark again. The examinations, labs, the pace of the work, and the whole system were different from my previous experience. I guess there is no escape from this. Survive the first term and things will get easier."

—*Giorgio Varsani, Italy (Medicine)*

"The best thing about this program is that it gives me the feeling of a real family. I feel as though I've made lifetime friends, and I know I'm not alone here. The other thing is that I've learned a lot about the culture. I've had the chance to experience the holidays and traditional foods, as well as the values here. For a newcomer, the program is really a good way to get used to a new situation quickly."

—*Alicia Carbajal, Colombia (Computer Programming)*

"New students should not expect the same kind of social life they had back home. How they get to know people and what kind of friends they make will be different here. Canadians are very friendly, but they have a high sense of duty and are therefore busy most of the time."

—*Mia Jun, Korea (English)*

Draw conclusions about the four students. Write the name of one student in each blank.

1. _____ must be living with a host family.
2. _____ must miss family and friends back home.
3. _____ must have taken morning and evening classes.
4. _____ must be comfortable living in different cultures.

Which student do you think has adapted most to the new culture? Least? On a separate piece of paper, write a paragraph stating and explaining your opinion.

Read the following comments that visitors to the United States have made about American customs and behavior. Complete the conclusions with *must* or *must not.*

1. Americans generally stand far away from each other when they talk. They
   (be) _____must not be_____ friendly people. In my country, people stand close together
   when they talk.

2. In the United States, employees call their employers by their first names. They
   (think) _____ that they are equals. In my country, employees call their
   bosses by their last name and use a title of respect.

3. In American schools, students usually do not stand up when their teacher enters the room.
   They *(respect)* _____ their teachers. In my country, students are
   required to stand up when a teacher enters the room.

4. American children usually do not live with their parents when they are over 18 years old.
   They *(love)* _____ their parents very much. In my country, children live
   with their parents until they get married.

5. Americans eat a lot of take-out food. They *(like)* _____ to cook. In my
   country, women usually cook a large meal every day.

Look at the paintings below. Then read the descriptions and write logical conclusions.

A.

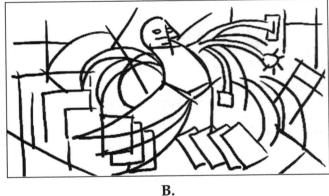

B.

1. This painting depicts continuous action with a series of overlapping figures.
   It must be painting B. It must not be painting A.

2. This painting creates a feeling of limitless space, a sense of peace and calm.

   _____

3. The artist who made this painting wanted to move away from traditional art forms.

   _____

Look at the pictures and write a logical conclusion for each one. Use some of the following expressions, or use your own.

| late | nervous | sick | battery/dead | single | hard |

1. <u>He must study hard.</u>

2. _____

3. _____

4. _____

5. _____

6. _____

Exercise **5**

Match the conclusions on the left with the reasons on the right. Use *must* or *must not* to complete the conclusions.

___d___   1. Lisa <u>must not</u> have a lot of free time

_____   2. Mr. Keen _____ be retired

_____   3. The comedy _____ be funny

_____   4. The woman _____ speak English

_____   5. Alice's parents _____ be proud of her

_____   6. The Castros _____ have a lot of money

_____   7. Jim _____ be afraid of flying

_____   8. Helen _____ be very disappointed

a. because I asked the question three times and she didn't answer me.

b. because they own a house in the country, an apartment in the city, and three cars.

c. because her boss said she couldn't take a vacation.

d. because she attends school from 8:00 to 2:00 and then works the night shift in the hospital.

e. because he commutes by plane every weekend.

f. because he's 70 years old, lives in Florida, and plays tennis every day.

g. because she got the leading role in the school play.

h. because the audience hasn't laughed at all.

UNIT 3

Lesson 1 She's washed the dishes.

Exercise 1

A family is going on vacation. Complete the conversations with tag questions and short answers based on the following list. (Completed tasks are marked with a ✔. Tasks that have not yet been completed are marked with an ✘.)

✔ clean out the refrigerator   ✔ ask post office to hold mail   ✘ lock windows and doors
✔ confirm the plane tickets   ✘ discontinue the newspaper   ✘ ask neighbors to check on
✘ pack the suitcases   ✔ get traveler's checks   house
✘ unplug major appliances   ✔ renew passport

1. **A:** You've confirmed the plane tickets, <u>haven't you?</u>
   B: <u>Yes, I have.</u>

2. **A:** You haven't packed the suitcases yet, _____
   B: _____

3. **A:** Rose has asked the post office to hold the mail, _____
   B: _____

4. **A:** Tommy hasn't discontinued the newspaper, _____
   B: _____

5. **A:** I haven't unplugged the major appliances yet, _____
   B: _____

6. **A:** You've cleaned out the refrigerator, _____
   B: _____

7. **A:** Alice has renewed her passport, _____
   B: _____

8. **A:** You haven't asked the neighbors to check on the house yet, _____
   B: _____

9. **A:** Tommy hasn't locked the windows and doors yet, _____
   B: _____

10. **A:** Alice and Tommy have gotten traveler's checks, _____
    B: _____

Look at Alice and Tommy's chores. Write tag questions and short answers.

	Alice	Tommy
1. wash the dishes	✔	✗
2. sweep the floor	✗	✔
3. take out the trash	✗	✔
4. make the bed	✔	✗
5. feed the cat	✗	✔
6. iron the clothes	✔	✗

1. Tommy hasn't washed the dishes yet, has he?
   No, he hasn't, but Alice has.

2. _____

3. _____

4. _____

5. _____

6. _____

Substitute *used to* for the underlined past tense verbs where it makes sense.

    I have learned many important lessons in my life. When I <u>was</u> young, I <u>thought</u> *(used to think)* that my

parents <u>were</u>₃ too old-fashioned. They <u>made</u>₄ a lot of rules for me and <u>didn't let</u>₅ me do many of

the things I <u>wanted</u>₆ to do. For example, my friends <u>stayed</u>₇ outside even after dark, but I <u>had to</u>₈

come in before dinner so I could help with the chores. Also, on weekends I <u>had to</u>₉ help my

parents in our family business. At the time, I <u>thought</u>₁₀ that my parents <u>were</u>₁₁ very unfair. But now

I realize that they <u>wanted</u>₁₂ me to learn about responsibility and being part of a family. Now that

I'm grown and have a family of my own, I appreciate the lessons I <u>learned</u>₁₃ from my parents, and

I'm trying to teach my own children those same lessons.

Write sentences comparing the past and the present. Use appropriate tenses.

1. Men got married when they were 22 years old. (now/26)
   <u>Men used to get married when they were 22 years old. Now they get married when</u>
   <u>they are 26 years old.</u>

2. Women stayed home to take care of their children. (now/go to work)
   _____

3. Women worked at traditionally "feminine" jobs. (now/in all professions)
   _____

4. Americans had large families. (now/small ones)
   _____

5. Most families lived in one place for a long time. (now/move more frequently)
   _____

===== **Exercise 5** =====

Complete these predictions about society in the future.

1. In twenty years, scientists <u>will find a cure for cancer.</u>
2. Fifty years from now, robots _____
3. When my great-grandchildren are born, the world population _____
   _____
4. In 150 years, space exploration _____
5. Twenty years from now, cars _____

Lesson 2   They were speaking too loudly.

The following sentences are good advice for someone who wants to be successful in getting a job. Complete each sentence with an appropriate adverb from the list below. There are many possible answers.

early	clearly	enthusiastically	carefully
politely	promptly	purposefully	logically
thoroughly	skillfully	professionally	well

1. To be ready for the interview, prepare <u>thoroughly</u> .
2. To make a good impression, dress _____ .
3. To avoid feeling nervous, arrive at the appointment _____ .
4. To sound confident, speak _____ .
5. To understand the job, listen to the interviewer _____ .
6. To be understood, answer questions _____ .
7. To show your interest, ask questions _____ .

In Exercise 1, you completed statements about how to be a successful job applicant. Can you think of some things that you *shouldn't* do? Complete these sentences about things a job applicant *shouldn't* do.

1. You shouldn't _____ *talk to the receptionist* _____ rudely.
2. You shouldn't _____ carelessly.
3. You shouldn't _____ too loudly.
4. You shouldn't _____ selfishly.
5. You shouldn't _____ too quickly.

Sometimes people have to deal with difficult job situations. Write a brief description of what happened in each situation. Use adverbs from this lesson or other adverbs you have learned.

1. <u>The students were speaking too loudly in the library.</u>

_____

_____

_____

2. _____

_____

_____

_____

Read the following concert review and answer the questions below.

Ali Farka Touré at the Fillmore
African Musician Gets Audiences on Their Feet

by Erin Smith

It was a warm San Francisco night, and we were headed for the Fillmore Theater to see Ali Farka Touré. The only thing I knew about him was that he was a musician from Mali, West Africa, and that my friend Howard had said that attending a Touré concert was like riding a dream wave. I was looking forward to it.

People from all ages and backgrounds were there. I saw young white professionals nervously polishing their glasses, teenagers of all shapes and sizes wandering around in baggy pants, and older African Americans in traditional costumes calling out to friends in line. Howard and I looked around happily. Howard has a feeling about crowds, and he gave this one an A+.

When the doors opened, we wandered inside and found seats. We were only sitting for a short time, however. Once Mr. Touré took the stage, the crowd jumped to their feet and were out on the dance floor. Howard was right; the West African rhythms got us going and it really was like riding a wave of beautiful sound. The music started out slowly, but soon we found ourselves dancing energetically as the beat picked up.

Mr. Touré's music made me think of American blues, but he clearly has roots in the traditions of his native Mali, where the artist learned to play his first instrument, the gurkel. He learned to play the guitar soon after, and now he writes and performs his own music. Check him out as soon as you can!

1. What is the main idea? _____
2. Who is Ali Farka Touré? _____
3. What kind of music does he play? _____
4. What kinds of people came to the concert? _____
5. What happened at the concert? _____

Now write a one-paragraph summary of the concert review on a separate sheet of paper. Use your answers to the questions to write complete sentences. Remember to use paragraph format when you write your summary. When you finish, check your summary for form and accuracy.

- Did you cover the main points in the review?
- Did you use paragraph format correctly?
- Did you proofread your paragraph for correct grammar and punctuation?

Lesson 3   She graduated with honors.

Exercise 1

Read these brief biographies of two famous women. Then write questions based on the underlined sections.

Helen Keller became blind and deaf <u>because of an illness she had when she was 1½ years old</u>. <u>When she was almost 10</u>, she began to learn how to speak, even though she hadn't heard speech since she became ill eight years before. Determined to go to college, Keller entered <u>Radcliffe College</u> in 1900. She graduated with honors at a time when few women graduated from college. Keller devoted her life to teaching people about the blind. <u>She wrote books and spoke widely about the special needs of blind and deaf people.</u>

1. How did Helen Keller become blind and deaf? _____

2. _____

3. _____

4. _____

Dr. Chien-Shiung Wu was born <u>on May 31, 1912</u>, in Liu Ho, China. She was accepted <u>to the prestigious National Central University of Nanking</u>, graduating in 1936. She then moved to the United States <u>to pursue graduate studies in physics at Berkeley</u>. Dr. Wu received her Ph.D. in 1940 and became widely known as an expert <u>on nuclear fission</u>. Dr. Wu is known as the "First Lady of Physics" <u>because she was able to prove that identical nuclear particles do not always act alike</u>. She thereby disproved a widely accepted "law" of physics. For her work, Dr. Wu was elected to <u>the U.S. National Academy of Sciences</u> and received <u>the National Medal of Science</u> in 1975. She also became the first woman ever to be awarded <u>an honorary doctorate in science</u> from Princeton.

1. _____

2. _____

3. _____

4. _____

5. _____

6. _____

7. _____

8. _____

Look at the following chronology of Rosa Parks and write her story in your notebook. Refer to the biographies of Helen Keller and Chien-Shiung Wu as models. Use the following paragraph as your introduction.

Rosa Louise McCauley Parks is one of the most esteemed African American women in the United States. She started the Montgomery, Alabama, bus boycott in 1955 by refusing to give up her seat to a white man. She has been considered the mother of the modern civil rights movement.

Date	Event
1913	Born in Tuskegee, Alabama
1918	Her father leaves the family.
1921	Moves to Montgomery with her mother
1932	Marries Raymond Parks, a barber
1932	Becomes active in the local chapter of NAACP (National Association for the Advancement of Colored People)
1955	Arrested for not giving up her bus seat to a white man; black people boycott the city bus company

Date	Event
1956	U.S. Supreme Court rules that segregation on the Montgomery buses is unconstitutional.
1957	Moves to Detroit with her mother and husband
1977	Her husband dies.
1987	Founds the Rosa and Raymond Parks Institute of Self-Development

Answer the following questions about yourself, and then write a short autobiography in your notebook. Give your autobiography an interesting title.

1. What's your name?
2. Where were you born?
3. Who are your parents? What do they do?
4. What were you like as a child? Did you have any unusual characteristics?
5. What were your dreams, goals, or ambitions when you were a child?
6. When did you start going to school?
7. What are your interests and hobbies?
8. What have you achieved so far in your life?
9. What are your goals for the future?
10. How do you feel about your life at this moment?

When you finish, check your paper.

- Does your paper have a title?
- Is there a margin at each side of the paper?
- Did you indent each paragraph?
- Does your paper have a main idea?
- Did you proofread for spelling, punctuation, capitalization, and grammar?

UNIT 4

Lesson 1 I wanted to learn new skills.

Exercise 1

Look at the pictures. Write sentences using *before* and *after*.

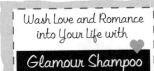   

1. Before she used Glamour Shampoo, she spent her evenings at home alone.

2. After she washed her hair with Glamour Shampoo, she was invited to every party in town.

3. _____

_____

4. _____

_____

5. _____

_____

6. _____

_____

7. _____

8. _____

═══════════ **Exercise 2** ═══════════

Look at the pictures and complete the paragraph below using *before*, *after*, **or** *when*.

Susana got up _____when_____ the alarm clock rang. _____ she ate
                        1   2

breakfast, she went jogging in the park. _____ she got home, it started to rain. She
                                                3

jogged home as fast as she could. The phone was ringing _____ she opened the
                                                                4

door. _____ she ran to answer it, she stepped on the cat's tail, and the cat jumped
           5

up onto the phone. _____ the cat knocked over the phone, it hit Susana on the head.
                           6

_____ she could answer the phone, it stopped ringing. Susana hoped her afternoon
       7

would be better than her morning had been!

Exercise 3

Read the following directions for making espresso coffee. They are not in the correct order. Number them so that they are in a logical order.

_____ Push the button that starts the machine.

_____ Fill the filter basket with espresso-grind coffee.

_____ Serve immediately.

___1___ Fill the machine's reservoir with cold, fresh water.

_____ Clamp the filter securely into the machine and place a cup underneath.

_____ Turn off the machine in about 20 seconds.

___2___ Plug in the machine.

On a separate piece of paper, write a paragraph describing how to make espresso. Use the list as a guide, adding more details if you wish. Be sure to use the signal words *before*, *when*, and *after*. Begin your paragraph with the following sentence:

After you fill the machine's reservoir with cold, fresh water, you plug in the machine.

Exercise 4

Look at the comments of five retired people. Match their comments to their reasons for working hard all their lives.

_____ 1. **Nguyen:** My family was the most important thing in my life. Everything I earned, I earned for them.

_____ 2. **Ana:** I didn't want to be a burden to my family when I retired. That's why I managed to put away a little money each month.

_____ 3. **Sean:** My goal was to have a penthouse in the city, a summerhouse at the seashore, and four or five race cars.

_____ 4. **Samuel:** Working kept me abreast of the latest technology in my field.

_____ 5. **Faye:** The position really helped my self-esteem and assertiveness.

a. Feel good about myself
b. Learn new skills
c. Save money for the future
d. Make lots of money
e. Provide for my family

On a separate piece of paper, write a paragraph about the people described above. Begin your paragraph with the sentence below.

In a recent survey, five of our retired workers expressed a wide variety of reasons for working. For example, Nguyen worked because he wanted to provide for his family.

Lesson 2 He said, "I have a toothache."

════════════ **Exercise 1** ════════════

Mark is taking his son, Sam, to see the dentist. Complete the conversations.

1. <u>Mark said to the man, "I've heard that</u> <u>this dentist is very good."</u>
_____
_____

2. <u>Sam said to his father, "</u> _____
_____ . "

<u>His father responded, "</u> _____
_____ . "

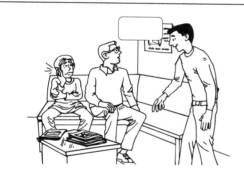

3. _____
_____
_____

4. _____
_____
_____

5. _____
_____
_____

6. _____
_____
_____

Look at the following statements and guess who might have said them. Then write a sentence telling what the person said.

1. Don't forget to stop by the cleaner's on your way home. My wife said, "Don't forget to stop by the cleaner's on your way home."

2. You get a 10 percent discount on all our paperback novels. _____

3. You were driving twenty miles over the speed limit. _____

4. Take one capsule in the morning and one after dinner. _____

5. You won't be able to find a lower price on a car like this anywhere in town. _____

6. Your journals are due next Monday. Also, don't forget to do the exercises in your workbook for Monday. _____

7. Walk slowly toward the camera while looking to your left. _____

8. You need to check out by noon; otherwise, you'll be charged for an extra night. _____

Complete the following conversation between Yumiko and a representative from a credit company with appropriate questions.

1. "_____?"
   "My first name is spelled Y-U-M-I-K-O, and my last name is spelled S-A-T-O."

2. "_____?"
   "I was born in 1980."

3. "_____?"
   "Yes, I have both a checking account and a savings account."

4. "_____?"
   "My driver's license number is C23471."

5. "_____?"
   "Yes, I do. I work for a publishing company."

Read Sofia's journal. Then complete the sentences with one of the following statements.

That's where I'm going. I'm traveling to Turkey next month. I'm from Turkey. What city are you from? For business. I'm going to be teaching English at a private school in Turkey.	Yes, I am. Are you going to Turkey for business or pleasure? Excuse me, I noticed you're reading a book about Turkey. May I ask you why? I'm from Istanbul. What can you tell me about Istanbul?

Yesterday, I was sitting in a coffee shop, studying for my test. At the table next to me was a woman reading a book about Turkey. I was very curious about why she was reading about my country, so I turned to her and asked, "Excuse me, I noticed that _____1_____ you're reading a book about Turkey. _____1_____ May I ask you why?" _____2_____ The woman smiled and said, " _____3_____ ."

I became even more curious. I asked, " _____4_____ ?"

She answered, " _____5_____ .

_____6_____ ."

"So, you're an English teacher?" She said, " _____7_____ ."

I said, " _____8_____ ."

She looked delighted to hear that. She asked, " _____9_____ ?"

I answered, " _____10_____ ."

She said, " _____11_____ ."

Then she asked, " _____12_____ ?"

I told her about all the interesting places she can visit in Istanbul and also gave her some tips on how to save money while living there. Before I left, I gave her my parents' phone number and told her to call them if she needed help.

Lesson 3 It's more fun than walking.

═══════════════════════ **Exercise 1** ═══════════════════════

Look at the pictures. Then read the sentences and circle *T* (true) or *F* (false).

Andres   **Miho**   **Mr. Xu**

1. Andres is as sick as Mr. Xu.   T   F
2. Andres and Miho are not as sick as Mr. Xu.   T   F
3. Miho's cold is not as bad as Andres's cold.   T   F
4. Andres's fever is as high as Miho's fever.   T   F
5. Mr. Xu's illness is more serious than Miho's.   T   F
6. Andres thinks his job is more important than his health. T   F

On the lines below, rewrite the false sentences, making them true.

_____

_____

_____

_____

_____

_____

What activities do you enjoy doing? State your opinion by circling the appropriate comparison. Then write three statements of your own about the activities listed in the chart.

Sports	Entertainment	Hobbies
• Playing soccer • Playing tennis • Swimming • Bicycle riding • Walking • Playing baseball	• Going to movies • Eating in a restaurant • Going to parties • Watching television • Dancing • Listening to music	• Building things • Drawing or painting • Playing a musical instrument • Collecting things • Cooking • Reading books

1. Playing team sports is (*more fun than / not as much fun as*) swimming.
2. Watching TV is (*more entertaining than / not as entertaining as*) listening to music.
3. Reading books is (*more pleasant than / not as pleasant as*) playing a musical instrument.
4. Going to parties is (*as enjoyable as / not as enjoyable as*) eating in a restaurant.
5. _____
6. _____
7. _____

What qualities do you look for when you choose a doctor? Compare the following qualities.

1. A popular doctor with a busy schedule or one who is available but unpopular?
   A popular doctor with a busy schedule is not as good as one who is available but unpopular.
   OR
   A popular doctor with a busy schedule is better than one who is available but unpopular.

2. Kind or efficient?
   _____

3. Young or experienced?
   _____

Compare the following occupations in terms of stress. Is one more stressful than the other, or are they the same? Write sentences explaining your choices.

1. a journalist/a firefighter

_____

_____

_____

2. a police officer/a truck driver

_____

_____

_____

3. a waiter/a cook

_____

_____

_____

4. a construction worker/an engineer

_____

_____

_____

Exercise 5

How would you describe yourself? Check one of the following statements.

_____ I am very serious about taking care of my health.

_____ I try to stay healthy, but I don't always do everything that I should.

_____ I don't worry a lot. When I get sick, I just go to the doctor.

Copy the statement that you checked on the lines below. Then write a short paragraph about your health habits. Give at least three examples.

_____

_____

_____

_____

_____

Lesson 1 I haven't been sleeping well.

Exercise 1

Look at the picture. Use the words in the box to write sentences about what the people in the picture have been doing. (The times indicate when each action began.)

eat   wait   talk   work   read   cry

1. The man has been talking on the phone since 7:10.
   OR The man has been talking on the phone for the past twenty minutes.
2. _____
3. _____
4. _____
5. _____
6. _____

Exercise 2

Read the following statements a classmate is making to you. Explain by telling what's been going on in your life.

1. Your eyes look red and puffy today.
   I haven't been sleeping well lately.

2. You sure have a lot of paint on your clothes.
   _____

3. You look like you're losing weight.
   _____

4. You haven't been spending much time relaxing with your friends lately.
   _____

5. You're coughing and sneezing a lot this week, aren't you?
   _____

6. You're doing very well on your tests lately.
   _____

Exercise 3

Suji, an English student, is talking with her new classmate, Leila. Leila wants to know what Suji has been doing to improve her English and to be a successful student. Complete their conversation with questions and answers.

Leila: So, how long have you been studying English here?

Suji: I've been studying English for the past two years.

Leila: _____?

Suji: _____.

Leila: _____?

Suji: _____.

Leila: _____

Suji: _____.

Leila: _____?

Suji: _____.

Suji is talking to her American friend, Julia. Complete their conversation with the correct forms of the verbs in parentheses.

Julia: Your English has improved a lot since the last time I saw you. How could that happen in such a short time?

Suji: Thank you for saying that! I (take) _____ a lot of English classes since we last saw each other.

Julia: I'm sure that's not the whole story. Learning a language takes more than just attending classes.

Suji: You're right. I (work) _____ on my English outside of class too.

Julia: Doing what?

Suji: Well, I (read) _____ English novels.

Julia: That's great. What are you reading now?

Suji: I'm reading a novel about an immigrant in the United States. It's a very interesting book.

Julia: So, I forget. (how long / study) _____ English? It's been a year or so, hasn't it?

Suji: Actually, it's been almost two years.

Julia: Wow! Time sure passes quickly! Guess what? I (learn) _____ Korean for a year now.

Suji: You're kidding! That's wonderful. (you / have) _____ many chances to practice your Korean?

Julia: Just one. I (correspond) _____ with a Korean pen pal by e-mail.

Suji: Has it been helpful?

Julia: Yes, it has, but I (not / be able to) _____ send a lot of e-mail lately because I just started a new job, and I (work) _____ ten hours a day.

Suji: You can practice your Korean with me if you want to. I'll give you my phone number, and we can call each other. But we have to speak English, too!

Julia: That'd be great. Thank you!

Lesson 2   Tyler's bed is made.

Look at the map of a local high school. Then complete each sentence with the correct form of the verb.

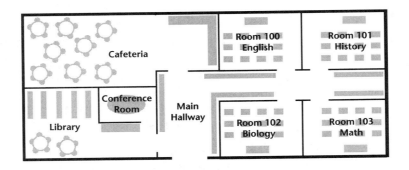

1. Math *(teach)* _____is taught_____ in Room 103.
2. The library *(locate)* _____ next to the cafeteria.
3. Conferences *(hold)* _____ in the library.
4. Biology *(teach)* _____ in Room 102.
5. Lunch *(serve)* _____ in the cafeteria.

Look at the signs and write a sentence explaining the meaning of each one.

1. _Smoking is not permitted._ _____

2. _____
   _____

3. _____
   _____

4. _____
   _____

Look at the two teenagers' rooms. Then write sentences describing each one.

| Tyler | Janie |

Tyler's room.

Example: <u>The bed is made.</u>

1. _____
2. _____
3. _____

Janie's room

Example: <u>The curtains are torn.</u>

4. _____
5. _____
6. _____

Exercise 4

Read the following pairs of sentences. Decide whether the active or passive voice is better for each context. Put a check next to the appropriate sentences and put an X next to the inappropriate sentences.

__X__ 1. People speak Portuguese in Brazil.   __✓__ Portuguese is spoken in Brazil.

_____ 2. A person stole my books last night!   _____ My books were stolen last night!

_____ 3. Mr. Drew knows the answer.   _____ The answer is known by Mr. Drew.

_____ 4. People raise cattle in Texas.   _____ Cattle are raised in Texas.

_____ 5. Nina loves chocolate.   _____ Chocolate is loved by Nina.

_____ 6. People are not allowed to park here.   _____ Parking is not allowed here.

Exercise 5

Complete the paragraph with the correct form of the verb. Decide whether each sentence should be active or passive and what tense you should use. Some sentences have more than one possible answer.

These days teenagers (give) _____ 1 a greater voice in U.S. society in many ways. First of all, they (have) _____ 2 a great deal of money to spend, so many advertisements (aim) _____ 3 directly at teens. Second, teenagers (think) _____ 4 about the world they will inherit. They are active in working for a better environment, and many cleanup campaigns (organize) _____ 5 by youth groups. Third, most teens (know) _____ 6 how to use computers, and many students are more highly skilled than their teachers or parents when it comes to using new technologies. Finally, a majority of teens (avoid) _____ 7 bad habits such as drinking and smoking. Athletics and good health (consider) _____ 8 to be very important by the average 13- to 19-year-old. Parents and other adults think these characteristics are a fine thing. They (expect) _____ 9 good things from the next generation.

Lesson 3 It's a little too warm.

Exercise 1

Carolyn and Ben are preparing for their daughter's wedding. Underline the state verbs in the questions. Then match the questions with the answers.

_b_ 1. Does the temperature <u>feel</u> OK?

___ 2. Does the soup taste good?

___ 3. How does Maria look?

___ 4. How does the music sound?

___ 5. How do the flowers smell?

a. No, it's too bland. I think it needs a little more salt.

b. We'd better make it cooler. We're expecting over 100 guests.

c. A little too fragrant. Why don't you open the windows a little?

d. She's as radiant as you were on our wedding day.

e. Very screechy! Don't we have another recording?

Find the sensory adjectives in the answers above. Write each one under the correct state verb in the boxes below.

look	sound	smell	taste	feel
				cool

Exercise 2

Here is a list of adjectives related to our five senses of sight, hearing, smell, taste, and touch. Match the adjective on the left with its definition on the right. Use the context of the questions and answers in Exercise 1 to help you.

___ 1. rough

___ 2. fragrant

___ 3. radiant

___ 4. delicious

___ 5. screechy

___ 6. smooth

___ 7. yelping

___ 8. musty

___ 9. gloomy

___ 10. bland

a. having a stale or moldy odor

b. high-pitched, harsh, piercing

c. having an even surface

d. not strong or distinctive in taste

e. dismal, dark, or dreary

f. having a pleasant odor; sweet-smelling

g. uneven, not smooth

h. greatly pleasing to the taste or palate

i. glowing, beaming, extremely happy

j. sharp, short barking or crying as in pain or surprise

Complete the conversations with the correct form of the verbs.

APARTMENT 204

1. A: I can't wear wide stripes. I *(look)*
   _____ too fat in them.

   B: I know what you mean. I *(have)*
   _____ the same
   problem.

APARTMENT 206

2. A: Shhh! Listen to that noise. It *(sound)*
   _____ scary.

   B: Oh, that's only the cat. She *(look for)*
   _____ a mouse.

APARTMENT 104

3. A: I *(feel)* _____ sick.

   B: Well, you should. You just ate two large
   pizzas all by yourself. You *(seem)*
   _____ pretty tired, too.

   A: Yeah, but I won't be able to sleep after
   eating all that pizza.

APARTMENT 106

4. A: Phew! This backpack *(smell)*
   _____ terrible. What's in
   it?

   B: Oh, no! I forgot to take out the fish I
   bought on the way home.

   A: No wonder the cat *(smell)*
   _____ it.

Betty and Brad are at a restaurant. Complete their conversation by circling the appropriate adjectives and adverbs.

Brad: You look (1. *beautiful / beautifully*) tonight, Betty.

Betty: Thanks, Brad. This is a great restaurant! The food tastes (2. *delicious / deliciously*), and the band sounds (3. *terrific/terrifically*).

Brad: Yeah. They really play (4. *superb / superbly*), don't they? Hey, would you like to dance?

Betty: You bet.

Brad: It feels (5. *delightful / delightfully*) to dance again. You know, I haven't danced with you since our wedding.

Betty: Be careful! Those people are really dancing (6. *bad / badly*).

Brad: You're right. They look (7. *dangerous / dangerously*).

Betty: Ouch, my toe! Let's sit down.

Brad: Good idea. How about some coffee? The people next to us just got some, and it smells (8. *wonderful / wonderfully*).

Betty: That sounds (9. *nice / nicely*). Let's order some dessert, too.

UNIT 6

Lesson 1 I'm comfortable with strangers.

Exercise 1

John, Roberto, and Mia took a social anxiety test. Look at their answers. Write the name of the person that matches each description below.

1 = almost never	2 = rarely	3 = sometimes	4 = quite often	5 = most of the time

	John	Roberto	Mia
1. I enjoy the company of other people.	5	2	4
2. I feel comfortable in a group of strangers.	4	1	4
3. I feel embarrassed when I have to speak in a small group of people.	1	5	3
4. I value introductions to people I don't know.	4	2	4
5. I hate crowds.	1	5	4
6. I like places where I can get to know new people.	5	1	4
7. I am at ease with people I don't know well.	5	1	5
8. I like conversations with strangers.	4	2	3
9. I hate situations in which I am expected to socialize.	1	5	3
10. I love unfamiliar social situations.	5	1	3

1. Your test score shows that you are quite uncomfortable in most social situations. You appear to have a number of weak social areas, and there are social situations that make you feel very nervous and unsure of yourself. A little work on your social skills will increase your self-esteem. _____

2. It looks like you are a real social animal! Your test score shows that you are comfortable in most social situations. You seem to be comfortable with complete strangers as well as with friends. Your ability to socialize and meet new people is extremely good. Keep it up.

_____

3. Your test score shows that you are relatively comfortable in some but not all social situations. You have a few weak spots, and there are situations that make you feel rather nervous and unsure of yourself. Working on these areas will help you fully enjoy your social life.

_____

Read the survey and answer the questions in complete sentences.

CONSUMER PRODUCT SURVEY

Dear Shopper:

Here's a simple statistic that may surprise you: 80% of all *NEW* products that come to market fail in a few short years. This means that a significant percentage of the products you use today will simply disappear from the marketplace, never to return again. Everything you buy, from laundry detergent to headache remedies, is critically dependent on one thing for its continued existence. That thing is your opinion. When you speak your mind, better products get to market. That's why it's so important for you to take a few minutes right now to complete the enclosed survey. In addition, your participation in the survey guarantees that you will continue to receive our valuable coupon mailings. Don't miss out!

Sincerely,

Aldo Rinaldi

National Sales Manager

- -

Name: _____   Age: _____   Occupation: _____

1. Where do you *live*? I live _____

2. Do you *prefer* to shop alone or with someone? _____
   _____

3. What do you *enjoy* shopping for? _____
   _____

4. What do you *hate* about shopping? _____
   _____

5. When you shop, do you *tend* to use a credit card? _____
   _____

6. Do you *understand* the terms of your credit card? _____
   _____

7. Do you *like* bargains? _____
   _____

8. When you buy a new car, what do you *consider*: the model, the price, or the quality?
   _____

9. Do you *remember* birthdays and anniversaries? _____
   _____

10. What do you *prefer* to receive as a gift: flowers, candy, clothing, or jewelry?
   _____

Exercise 3

Complete these sentences with the correct form of the verb.

1. *(think)* Mr. Rinaldi _____ consumers' opinions are important. He _____ about sending out a consumer product survey.

2. *(see)* Mr. Rinaldi _____ the marketing director about conducting a consumer survey. He _____ a need for consumer participation.

3. *(understand)* Mr. Rinaldi _____ the importance of consumer surveys.

4. *(hate)* He _____ consumers to miss out on the coupon mailings.

Exercise 4

Proofread this draft of an essay about Professor Haro's student profiles. Find and correct the eight errors in the essay. (The first one has been done for you.) Then match the students' pictures with their profiles. Write the students' names under their pictures.

1. _____   2. _____   3. _____   4. _____

                   is writing

Professor Haro ~~writes~~ profiles of his students today. He writes them every month. He is understanding his students and knows their strengths and weaknesses.

- John is loving independent work and hands-on activities. He has difficulty with routine and structured presentations. He is liking immediate results and learns by doing.

- Maria, on the other hand, is wanting rules and directions. She enjoys a structured environment. She is understanding the responsibilities and duties of the classroom.

- Mia values authenticity and honesty and enjoys close relationships. It is important that her classmates are valuing her as a person and that they listen to her opinions and respect her feelings.

- Roberto prefers independent work. He is enjoying new ideas and new concepts. He needs immediate challenges. He likes to discover solutions to problems and respects knowledge and capability.

Lesson 2 They'd rather travel together.

================== Exercise **1** ==================

Look at the pictures showing the young people's preferences. Then write a sentence using
would rather (*'d rather*) for each picture.

1. He'd rather be at the beach with his friends. He'd rather not be cleaning the garage.

2. _____

3. _____

4. _____

5. _____

6. _____

Answer the following questions about your vacation preferences.

1. Would you rather travel in the winter or in the summer?

   _____

2. Would you rather spend your vacation enjoying nature or exploring a famous city?

   _____

3. Would you prefer to travel by train, bus, or plane?

   _____

4. Would you rather travel alone or with someone else?

   _____

5. Would you prefer to have a tour guide show you around or to discover the attractions of a city on your own?

   _____

======= **Exercise 3** =======

Write one or two sentences describing what the person in each of the following situations *had better* ('d better) do.

1. Nguyen has a test tomorrow, but he's playing computer games.
   <u>He'd better study for the test. He'd better not play computer games anymore today.</u>

2. Carlos received a low grade on his last test.

   _____

3. Maria has to pass the TOEFL® in order to enter a university in the United States.

   _____

4. Ali can't see the chalkboard because he's sitting in the back row.

   _____

5. Yoko has a lot of spelling errors in her compositions.

   _____

6. Davida always forgets what her homework assignments are.

   _____

Exercise 4

Read each set of goals and options. Decide which option would help you meet the goal. Write a sentence for each goal using *I'd rather*, *I'd better*, and *because*.

1. Goal: to save money   Options: eat at home or eat in a restaurant

   I'd rather eat at a restaurant, but I'd better eat at home because I want to save money.

2. Goal: not to be late for class   Options: go to bed early or go to bed late

   _____

3. Goal: to do well on the test   Options: spend the weekend with my friends or study for the test

   _____

4. Goal: to be close to my family   Options: study English in the United States or study English in my country

   _____

5. Goal: to improve my English quickly   Options: speak English in class or speak my native language in class

   _____

6. Goal: to get some exercise   Options: walk to school or drive to school

   _____

Exercise 5

Marco, Fernando, and Paolo are high school students. Complete their conversation with *had better* or *would rather*. Use contractions if possible.

Marco: What are your plans for this weekend? Are you going to the beach with us on Saturday?

Fernando: No, I don't think so. I _____ (1) stay home and work on my paper, or I'll never finish it.

Paolo: Oh come on! _____ (2) you _____ be working at your desk or having fun in the sun with us?

Fernando: I _____ (3) be with you, of course, but I _____ (4) not.

Marco: You're really disciplined! I can't study on Saturdays, especially in the evening.

Fernando: Well, I _____ (5) go out and party on the weekends than stay home and study. But this Saturday, I _____ (6) stay home.

Marco: OK, we _____ (7) go. We promised to help Tina set up her e-mail account.

Fernando: Take it easy. We'll get together next weekend.

Lesson 3   She likes to read books.

Exercise 1

Look at the Leon family portrait. Then answer the questions using *and* or *but*.

1. How is Tatiana different from her husband, Ricardo?

   Tatiana likes to read books, but Ricardo prefers to take photographs.

2. How is Sara different from her younger sister, Rebecca?

   _____

3. How is Tatiana similar to her daughter Sara?

   _____

4. How is Rebecca similar to her father?

   _____

5. How is Ricardo different from his daughter Sara?

   _____

6. How is Rebecca different from her mother?

   _____

Write two sentences comparing yourself with two different members of your family.

7. _____

   _____

8. _____

   _____

Where does each member of the Leon family prefer to spend Saturday afternoons? Look at the pictures and write sentences using *so*.

1. She likes to read, so she stays at home.

2. _____

3. _____

4. _____

Proofread the paragraph that Sara Leon wrote about her family and put in any missing commas and periods. Then answer the questions below.

> All family members have some similarities and some differences. My family and I like spending time together but we like to spend time with our hobbies, too. My mother and I are bookworms We like to read books so we spend a lot of time indoors My mother reads novels and I study for school. On the other hand, my father and my sister like to spend time outdoors He likes to take photographs and my sister loves to play soccer They spend a lot of time in the sun so they are both very tan and strong. Sometimes I think that we do not look like we are from the same family but we are all Leons. We just have different characteristics.

1. What is the main idea of the paragraph?

   _____

2. What are the two main supporting details?

   a. _____
   b. _____

3. What are the concluding ideas?

   _____

   _____

Write notes about your mother, your father, and yourself in the boxes. Then complete the writing activity below.

Your mother	Your father	Yourself
How does she like to spend her time?	How does he like to spend his time?	How do you like to spend your time?

Are you more similar to your mother or to your father? Write a sentence explaining who you are more like. This sentence should express the main idea of your paragraph. It will be the topic sentence for the paragraph you will write below.

_____

_____

Now write a paragraph comparing yourself with the parent you are most similar to. Start your paragraph with the topic sentence you wrote. Add supporting details using your notes in the boxes. Be sure to add a conclusion.

_____

_____

_____

_____

_____

_____

_____

When you finish, proofread your paragraph.

- Does your paragraph have a topic sentence?
- Does your paragraph have supporting details?
- Did you indent the first sentence?
- Did you use commas and periods correctly?
- Did you capitalize the first word of every sentence?
- Does your paragraph have a conclusion?

UNIT 7

Lesson 1 Are you happy with your job?

======== **Exercise 1** ========

Alice and Masoud are expecting their first baby. Look at the pictures and write sentences describing who *is supposed to* do each of the things that they have to do before the baby arrives.

buy furniture	see the doctor every week
✔ paint the baby's room	eat healthy food
buy baby clothes	learn about raising a child

1. He's supposed to paint the baby's room.

2. _____

3. _____

4. _____

5. _____

6. _____

Write about what Alice and Masoud *are not supposed to* do after the baby arrives.

1. They are not supposed to leave the baby alone at home.
2. _____
3. _____
4. _____
5. _____

Exercise 2

Yoko, a mother of two, has a part-time job in a bank. She is talking with her friend Yoshie about the promotion she has been offered. Complete their conversation.

Yoko: This new position would be a great promotion, but if I *(take)* _____took_____ it, I'd have to work full-time and leave my children at daycare.

Yoshie: But if you *(accept)* _____ it, you'd make more money.

Yoko: Money isn't everything. My children are the most important thing to me.

Yoshie: Yes, I feel the same way about mine. Could you work part-time in the new position? If they really *(want)* _____ you, they'd let you do that.

Yoko: This position comes with a lot of responsibilities, so even if they *(allow)* _____ me to work part-time, I wouldn't accept it.

Yoshie: You need to do what works for you, but if I *(be)* _____ you, I'd take the job.

Yoko: How about you? Are you happy with your job?

Yoshie: Not really. In fact, I'm thinking about a change of career, too.

Exercise 3

Yoshie has made the following chart to help her analyze her career options. First complete the chart. Then write a sentence describing each option.

Career option	Pros	Cons
Teach retail merchandising at the local college	Good medical benefits, flexible schedule, long vacations	Low salary, many papers to grade
Become a travel agent		
Get a master's degree in business administration		
Quit my job and stay home with the children		
Stay in my present job as department store manager		

1. If she were a teacher, she'd have flexible working hours, but her salary would be low.

2. _____

3. _____

4. _____

5. _____

Exercise 4

Read about Yoshie and Yoko's current situations. Then write hypothetical sentences beginning with *if*. (Remember that the *if*-clause describes the condition.)

1. Yoshie isn't happy with her current job, so she wants to change her career.
   If Yoshie were happy with her current job, she wouldn't want to change her career.

2. Yoko won't accept the promotion because she wants to spend time with her children.
   If Yoko didn't want to spend time with her children,

3. Yoko won't make more money because she won't accept the promotion.
   _____

4. Yoshie has some extra money in the bank, so she can afford to consider different options.
   _____

5. Life is exciting because there are so many choices.
   _____

Exercise 5

One way to get rich, and perhaps not work, is to win the lottery. Read this selection from the book *The Lucky Winners*. Then answer the questions that follow.

Everybody thinks I am the luckiest person in the world. Why? Because a couple of months ago, I won $10 million in the lottery. In fact, I felt extremely fortunate when I realized that I was $10 million richer. But my excitement didn't last long. As soon as my friends and relatives heard the news, they visited me more often. Some of them started complaining about their financial problems without asking for money directly. Others were more direct. My brother wanted to borrow some money to fix his roof, and my cousin badly needed a car.

Another problem I faced after winning the lottery was more personal. I had never had so much money, so I didn't have any idea what to do with it. Of course, everybody had some advice on what to do with the money, and I received tons of brochures from various investment companies. Finally, to deal with all this in a more relaxed environment, I decided to take a vacation at a private resort in the mountains. While on vacation, I made the most important decision in my life.

1. How would you feel if you won the lottery?
   _____

2. How would you react if your relatives asked to have some of the money?
   _____

3. Would your life be easier if you won the lottery? Why?
   _____

4. What do you think the lottery winner's decision was?
   _____

Lesson 2   I enjoy helping people.

Read the classified ads and complete the conversations with the correct form of the verbs used in the ads.

555-4492 to schedule an appointment.

PATIENT CARE ASSOCIATE
Requires high school diploma and two years nurse's aide experience. Must communicate effectively in English. Bilingual preferred. Must be able to work independently without close supervision. Full-time position. Excellent pay plus opportunity for overtime work. Fax résumé to Human Resources at (281) 555-9339

1 bedroom apartment in a doorman building. $500 mo., call 555-7989 No pets allowed.

---

that reads "Henry." Family is heartbroken. Please call (281) 555-3929.

CIVIL ENGINEERS
8 years minimum experience in design and management of urban construction projects for streets, bridges, utility systems, and storm sewers. Good communication, planning, and organizational skills are essential. Long-term employment, excellent benefits. Call (713) 555-4492 to schedule an appointment.

PATIENT CARE ASSOCIATE

---

résumé to Human Resources at (281) 555-9339

WORD PROCESSING COORDINATOR
Supervise the activities of our team of Word Processors. Responsibilities include scheduling work and training new employees. At least 1 year in a supervisory position. Strong analytical ability, PC proficiency, and knowledge of networked desktop systems are a must. For immediate consideration, please forward a résumé to Bowie Business Solutions, 602 Sawyers, Houston, TX 77007

ENTRY-LEVEL ACCOUNTANTS
Company hiring accounting graduates with 0–4 years experience. The ideal candidate will be detail-oriented and enjoy working with numbers. Experience taking inventory a plus. Excellent opportunity. Full benefits package, including pension plans. Please send your résumé and salary requirements to: SEALY, 2601 Spenwick Drive, Houston TX 77044. No phone calls.

---

1. **A:** Can you tell me a little about the Patient Care Associate position, please?

   B: Well, the Patient Care Associate must enjoy ___communicating___ effectively in English. The candidate should like _____ independently without close supervision. He or she can anticipate _____ overtime.

2. **A:** I would like some information about the Civil Engineer position, please.

   B: Of course. We're looking for a person who likes _____ and _____ urban construction projects for streets, bridges, utilities, and storm sewers. The applicant must appreciate _____ with colleagues and _____ work schedules.

3. **A:** Could you please explain the Word Processing Coordinator position?

   B: I'd be glad to. The person must enjoy _____ the activities of a team of word processors. He or she must not mind _____ work and _____ new employees.

4. **A:** I'm calling about the Accountant position.

   B: Yes, this is an entry-level position. The company is recommending _____ two or three recent graduates. Candidates should enjoy _____ with numbers and _____ inventory.

You are the personnel officer in charge of hiring a new salesperson for your company. Look at Paul Hall's and Stacy Trust's responses to the job questionnaire. Write a memo to the personnel director with your recommendation.

Job Questionnaire

How do you feel about the following job related responsibilities?

4 = love   3 = like   2 = don't like   1 = strongly dislike

	Paul	Stacy
1. helping people	2	4
2. working alone	4	1
3. having a lot of responsibility	2	3
4. working in an office	4	1
5. answering the telephone	3	2
6. traveling	1	4
7. writing letters	3	2
8. talking in front of many people	1	4

MEMO

To: Ms. Peters, Personnel Director
From: _____
Date: _____
Re: New sales position _____

   After carefully considering the two candidates, I recommend _____ for the position sales in our company. My reasons are the following:

   Stacy Trust _____
_____
_____
_____

   In contrast, Paul Hall _____
_____
_____
_____
_____

Complete this job questionnaire for a retail sales position. Use your own information.

JOB QUESTIONNAIRE: RETAIL SALESPERSON

How do you feel about these things? Check the appropriate box.

	LOVE	LIKE	DON'T LIKE	STRONGLY DISLIKE
1. meeting new people	☐	☐	☐	☐
2. wearing a suit	☐	☐	☐	☐
3. staying at home	☐	☐	☐	☐
4. learning new things	☐	☐	☐	☐
5. speaking other languages	☐	☐	☐	☐
6. working overtime	☐	☐	☐	☐
7. providing customer service	☐	☐	☐	☐
8. having a routine	☐	☐	☐	☐

Now, on a separate sheet of paper, write a cover letter applying for the sales position. Use your responses to the job questionnaire.

Dear Sir or Madam:

This letter is in response to your job advertisement in yesterday's *Daily News*.

_____

_____

_____

_____

Read this letter from Stacy's friend. There are ten mistakes in it. Find and correct them. (The first one has been done for you.)

Dear Stacy,

I just received your last letter. Congratulations! You must ~~to~~ be very happy with your new job! I know you have always enjoyed to work in sales. This job sounds perfectly for you.

I still hate my job. I can't stand be in the office all day. I enjoy to travel, and I want to meet new people. Perhaps one day I could to be a travel agent. I am thinking I'm good at talking to people, but I still need to improve my English. I don't like do the same thing every day. I hate follow routines, but I don't mind to have a lot of responsibility.

Well, I have to go to the store before it closes. Give my love to your family.

Lesson 3   I'd like to get a good job.

Mai is trying to find a job that will fit her school schedule. Look at the choices below. Then complete the conversation between Mai and her friend Marie with *too* or *very*.

Mai: I'm having a ___very___ hard time finding a good job. The jobs I want are ___too___ hard to
                                  ₁   ₂
      get without a college degree. So I'm looking for part-time work while I study.

Marie: What about working in a restaurant? I hear you can make very good money waiting on
       tables.

Mai: No, I can't do that. Waitressing is _____ stressful.
                                                  ₃

Marie: Well, you like exercise. Would you like to be a bicycle messenger?

Mai: Hmm, bicycle messengers are in _____ good shape, but that kind of work is _____
                                           ₄   ₅
       dangerous. I might get hit by a car.

Marie: I know it's _____ hard to decide, but you'll have to think of something.
                                                 ₆

Mai: I think I'll try to get a data-entry job at the college. It'll probably be a _____ boring job,
                                                                           ₇
       but it won't be _____ difficult. Besides, I'll be _____ close to my classes.
                            ₈   ₉

Exercise 2

Read the job announcement from Student Services and Mai's list of requirements below. Check the requirements that the job would fulfill.

> **WORK-STUDY JOBS ON CAMPUS**
> Student Services in the Administration Building needs part-time help with data entry. The applicant must have some computer experience, but training is available for work-study students. The hours are flexible, but the applicant must be willing to work at least 20 hours per week. Call 619-4556 for further information.

1. _____ I must have enough free time to study, especially during final exams.
2. _____ I would like to earn enough money to have my own apartment.
3. _____ I would love to be close enough to walk from my class to my job.

Exercise 3

Look at the pictures and complete the description of each situation.

1. Jane doesn't have enough money, so she can't buy a new computer.

2. Fred is very late, so _____

3. Tina spent too much time playing soccer, so _____

4. Haru didn't get enough sleep last night, so _____

Mai and Trey have both applied for work-study jobs. Read about how they prepared for the job interview. Then write an explanation of who you think will get the job and why.

Trey:
I went to bed late.
I didn't hear the alarm.
I arrived at the interview late.

Mai:
I went to bed early.
I set the alarm for 6:00 A.M.
I arrived at the interview early.

_____
_____
_____
_____
_____

Exercise 5

Read what Trey has written in his journal about his dream job. Then write about a dream job of your own.

> If I worked really hard, I could save enough money to buy a coffee cart. If the coffee business did well, I might have enough money to open a restaurant. If there were enough customers in my restaurant, I would open more restaurants. Soon I would have enough money to buy a big house and a nice car. Then, if I hired other people to manage my restaurants, I would have enough time to travel and do all the other things I dream about doing. But first, I need to get a job.

_____
_____
_____
_____

UNIT 8

Lesson 1 You'd better drive more slowly.

Exercise 1

Look at the signs below. Then write two sentences about each one using the contracted forms of *had better* and *had better not*.

1. You'd better not smoke in here.
   You'd better put out your cigarette.

2. _____

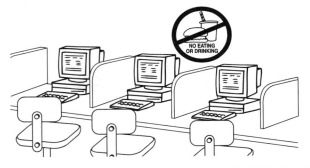

3. _____

4. _____

5. _____

6. _____

Use gerunds to complete the sentences describing the signs in Exercise 1.

1. _____Smoking_____ is not allowed in this restaurant.
2. _____ is prohibited in the swimming pool area.
3. _____ is not allowed in the computer lab.
4. _____ in the river is strictly prohibited.
5. _____ is illegal in the park.
6. _____ a dog without a leash is prohibited.

Exercise 3

Suji has just bought her first car. She is talking with the host of a radio car show, asking questions about the maintenance of her used car.

Suji: My name is Suji. I just bought my first used car, and I have some questions for you.

Host: Congratulations, Suji. How can I help you?

Suji: Well, there isn't anything wrong with my car. I just want to know how to maintain it.

Host: OK. First, make sure the oil is changed every 3,000 miles. This will protect your engine. Also, have the air filter checked every time you take your car in for an oil change. This way, you can save on gas and prevent major damage to your car.

Suji: Is there anything I can do myself to prevent expensive repairs?

Host: Sure. You should wash your car every now and then to protect the paint and prevent rust. Also, you can buy a tire pressure gauge and check your tires every time you put gas in your car. Doing that will lengthen the life of your tires. Finally, take your car in for a complete checkup once a year. It can save you a lot of money in the long run.

Suji: Thank you very much for your help.

Complete the following sentences based on the advice the host gave Suji on page 65.

1. _____Changing the oil_____ regularly will protect your car's engine.
2. _____ can save you money on gas.
3. _____ protects the paint and prevents rust.
4. _____ will lengthen the life of your tires.
5. _____ can save you a lot of money in the long run.

Exercise 4

Suji has had her car for a couple of months now. Read about each problem and make a suggestion from the following list. Use *should* or *had better*.

contact your car dealer	balance your tires	have your brakes checked
call some other companies	change your air filter	add coolant to the radiator

1. My car makes noise when I brake.
   You should have your brakes checked. They may need to be replaced.

2. My car insurance is too high. I can't afford it.
   _____

3. My car gets poor gas mileage.
   _____

4. I've lost the owner's manual for my car.
   _____

5. The car pulls to one side when I'm driving on the freeway.
   _____

6. The engine overheats in slow traffic.
   _____

Read the following statements about cars and driving. Then express your opinion by completing the sentences with *should* or *shouldn't*.

1. Car insurance for teenagers _____ be higher than for adults.
2. People _____ be required to buckle their seat belts.
3. There _____ be speed bumps in neighborhood streets.
4. Cars _____ be allowed in the downtown area.
5. There _____ be speed limits on freeways.
6. The government _____ limit the number of cars a family can have.

Exercise 6

Suji got a traffic ticket for speeding. Read the following remarks made by different people and complete them with *should, shouldn't, had better ('d better),* or *had better not ('d better not)* depending on the relationship between Suji and the speaker.

Police officer: You _'d better_ drive more slowly, or you may lose your driver's license next time.
                                      1

Suji's friend: You _____ always be on the lookout for a police car. You _____ buy
                                  2   3
a radar detector!

Suji's mother: You _____ drive more carefully, or you'll have an accident.
                                  4

Suji's brother: You _____ drive so fast. A freeway isn't a race track, you know.
                                   5

Suji: I _____ be more careful. I don't want to get any more tickets.
                           6

Lesson 2   I'm good at remembering things.

=== **Exercise 1** ===

Nanci's car was stolen, and she is thinking about buying a bicycle. Complete her conversation with her friend Vic with question expressions from the box below.

| How far | How much | How many | How expensive | How early | How soon |

Nanci: I don't think I really need a car. __How expensive__ is a good bike?

1

Vic: That depends on the bike. _____ do you travel each day?

2

Nanci: Not far, a few miles.

Vic: _____ hills do you expect to climb?

3

Nanci: There is one steep hill. So I guess I need a bike with good gears.

Vic: _____ money do you want to spend?

4

Nanci: Not more than $500.

Vic: _____ do you need it? I think there's a sale at the Bicycle Barn next week. I bet

5
we could find you one there.

Nanci: Perfect. I get paid on Friday. Let's go Saturday morning. _____ can you pick

6
me up?

Exercise 2

Read the statistics on car thefts. Then complete the sentences below.

Car Thieves Strike When Cars Left Running in Winter

Over Half of All Car Thefts Occur at Night

50% of All Stolen Vehicles Left Unlocked

Keys Left in the Ignition of 13% of All Stolen Vehicles

Source: Pennsylvania Automobile Theft Prevention Authority
http://www.watchyourcar.org/menu.html

1. You can prevent your car from being stolen by ___keeping it in your garage at night.___
2. If you don't leave your car running, you can discourage car thieves from _____
   _____
3. You can lower your chances of having your car stolen by _____
   _____
4. You can keep your car safe if you insist on _____
   _____

Exercise 3

Read each question and circle *Yes* or *No* to find out if you are forgetful.

1. Are you bad at remembering detailed information?   Yes   No
2. Do you get so involved in doing things that you forget the time?   Yes   No
3. Have you ever had to apologize for forgetting someone's name?   Yes   No
4. Were you ever guilty of forgetting to keep a promise?   Yes   No
5. Are you known for losing things?   Yes   No

If you answered *Yes* to three or more questions, then your friends might think you are absent-minded. Explain why you think you are or are not absent-minded. Give examples to support your opinion.

Example: I am absent-minded. I am terrible at remembering my car keys.

_____
_____
_____
_____

Look at the pictures and write a conversation between the police officer and the driver.

1.

2.

3.

4.

An elephant sat on it.

Officer: _____

Driver: _____

Officer: _____

Driver: _____

Officer: _____

Driver: _____

Officer: _____

Have you ever been in an accident? Write a description of what happened.

_____
_____
_____
_____
_____

Lesson 3   It's fun to give parties.

Read the newspaper article and answer the questions below.

Sunday May 7, 2000   *THE LOCAL HERALD*   C-1

---

1. _____

    Mothers Against Drunk Driving is a nonprofit grassroots organization with more than 600 chapters nationwide. MADD is not a crusade against alcohol consumption. Its focus is to look for effective solutions to the problems of drunk driving and underage drinking, while supporting those who have already experienced the pain of these senseless crimes.

2. _____

    MADD was founded by a small group of California women in 1980 after a 13-year-old-girl was killed by a hit-and-run driver. The driver had been involved in another hit-and-run drunk-driving crash and had three previous drunk-driving arrests and two convictions. He had been released from jail only two days before killing the little girl. He was sentenced to jail for two years but allowed to serve time in a work camp and later a halfway house.

3. _____

    Those injured and killed in drunk driving collisions are not "accident" victims. A crash caused by an impaired driver involves two choices: to drink AND to drive. The deaths and injuries caused each year by impaired driving can be prevented. They are not "accidental."

4. _____

    Since 1980, more than 1,600 laws against drunk driving have been enacted nationwide. Fifty states have adopted 21 as the standard legal drinking age. Two-thirds of the states have now passed administrative license revocation laws. These allow the arresting officer to take the driver's license of those who fail or refuse to take a breath test. More than a dozen states have passed "zero tolerance" laws, which prohibit those under 21 from having any measurable amount of alcohol in their blood stream.

Source: http://madd.org/aboutmad/default.shtml

1. Write the correct heading on the line above each paragraph.

        Drunk Driving Is Not an Accident   **What Is MADD?**
        Making a Difference   **MADD's History**

2. What does MADD stand for? _____

3. A *grassroots* organization is one that is started by _____.

    a. ordinary people   b. the government   c. farmers   d. mothers

Complete the following passage with the appropriate form of the verbs given.

Here is some good advice for making sure that your guests will have fun at your next party. First, it is fundamental *(invite)* _____ guests who are compatible so that no one feels

1
left out of the crowd. It is common *(plan)* _____ lots of group activities. And, of

2
course, it is essential *(prepare)* _____ plenty of food. However, it is a good idea

3
(avoid) _____ a lot of salty snacks so that people won't get too thirsty.

4

Next, it is vital *(ask)* _____ guests to appoint designated drivers before the

5
evening begins. It is also important *(offer)* _____ a variety of nonalcoholic beverages.

6
It is really helpful *(serve)* _____ a great dessert treat with coffee 90 minutes before

7
the party ends.

Finally, you can make it fun *(follow)* _____ these rules. For example,

8
it is easy *(hold)* _____ a contest for guests to create nonalcoholic drink recipes. It's

9
amusing *(serve)* _____ the winners' drinks at the party. Remember, it's not necessary

10
(drink) _____ at a party to have a good time.

11

Source: http://www.madd.org./programs/safe_party.html

Make a "to do" list for a party. Include some suggestions from the passage as well as some of your own.

1. Invite compatible people. _____
2. _____
3. _____
4. _____
5. _____
6. _____
7. _____
8. _____
9. _____
10. _____
11. _____
12. _____

Look at the following suggestions for using a "word bag" to help you build up your vocabulary.

(1) When you find a new word that you want to learn, write it down, cut it out, and stick it on a piece of cardboard. (2) Look at the word and try to recall the sentence it was in and its meaning. (3) Create mental pictures or associations to help you remember it. (4) Be imaginative! (5) Keep the word in a "word bag." This can be a cloth bag or even your pocket. (6) Later, take out a card, look at the word on the card, and try to recall its meaning. (7) You will probably find that your picture or association will help you. (8) Keep a separate record of each word in its original context so that you can check to see if you were right. (9) Don't use a dictionary unless you really have to.

Rewrite the paragraph by following these directions. Omit the numbers.

- In (1) use *it's essential* after *learn*.
- Begin (2) with *It is fundamental.*
- Begin (3) with *It's helpful.*
- Combine (3) and (4) with *and above all.*
- Begin (5) with *It is important.*
- In (6) use *it's fun* after *Later.*
- Begin (8) with *Finally, it is necessary.*
- Begin (9) with *It's better.*

When you find a new word that you want to learn, it's essential to write it down, cut it out, and stick it on a piece of cardboard.

Read the following suggestions for taking care of a computer. Then write a paragraph about computer care. Use some of the expressions you learned in Exercise 3.

Keep it in a cool place.
Keep it away from sunlight.
Keep drinks away from it.
Keep it free of dust.

Clean it with a slightly damp cloth.
Don't clean it with a chemical cleaner.
Don't turn it on and off quickly.

Here is some good advice for taking good care of your computer. First of all, it is essential to keep it in a cool place.

UNIT 9

Lesson 1 They plan to get married.

Exercise 1

Read the letter Samantha wrote to "Mr. Advice" and his response to her. Then answer the questions.

Tuesday, May 15, 2001	THE LOCAL HERALD	D-1

Dear Mr. Advice:
   I need help. My married sister lives in Chicago, and I would like to visit her, but I don't know how to get the money for the trip. My parents give me an allowance of $5 a week, and I want to go by next summer. My sister said she would pay for half the ticket. My question is what can I do to earn the rest of the money for a round-trip ticket to Chicago by next summer? A ticket costs $300.
                 Samantha, 13 years old

Dear Samantha:
   The easiest and quickest way to earn money for your trip is to collect cans to recycle. Ask all your friends and neighbors if you can have their aluminum cans to recycle. Most places will give you 5 cents per can, and that adds up rather quickly.
   Another way to raise money is to ask your neighbors if you can walk their dogs. If you charge $1 a day per dog, you'll have your plane ticket in no time at all.
   I hope these suggestions help you. Let me know if you need any more. Have a nice trip!
                    Mr. Advice

1. If her sister pays $150 for the plane ticket, how much does Samantha have to save?
   If her sister pays $150, Samantha has to save $150.

2. How much can Samantha save if she saves all of her allowance for three months?
   _____

3. How many cans should Samantha collect for recycling if she wants to earn $25?
   _____

4. If Samantha walks two dogs for thirty days, how much money can she earn?
   _____

Exercise 2

Match the part of the sentence on the left with the part on the right.

_____ 1. If she plans to go by plane,

_____ 2. If she calls her sister's family after 11:00 P.M.,

_____ 3. She should pay by May 31

_____ 4. She might miss the plane

_____ 5. If it rains very hard,

a. they might be asleep.

b. if she doesn't arrive at least an hour before takeoff.

c. the plane may not be able to land.

d. she should reserve the tickets in advance.

e. if she wants to get a good airfare.

Combine the comments of Speaker A and Speaker B to make sentences of advice.

A: We want to buy a new car.

B: You should look in the classified ads section of the *Times*.

1. If you want to buy a new car, you should look in the classified ads section of the Times.

A: He's thinking about traveling to China.

B: He can make his reservations through Ho Travel Agency.

2. _____

A: I love trying out new recipes from foreign countries.

B: You should subscribe to *International Cuisine* magazine.

3. _____

A: My parents really enjoy musical comedies.

B: They ought to buy season tickets to Playhouse in the Park.

4. _____

A: I want to impress Ana on our first date.

B: You should take her to a romantic French restaurant.

5. _____

A: My nephew is interested in astronomy.

B: He might want to join the Star Gazers Club.

6. _____

Complete Patricia's letter to Maria with the correct form of the verbs in the box.

give	find	live
come	get married	see
do	have	tell

Dear Maria,

Congratulations! I'm so happy for you. I think it's great that you and Rob plan ___to get married___ . Of course,
                                                                                              1

Sam and I promise _____ to the wedding! In fact, we can't wait _____ you again. It's
                        2   3

been a long time!

Where do you expect _____ after you get married? Is Rob's place big enough or will you have
                          4

_____ a new apartment?
    5

I remember when I got married. Setting up a household can be difficult. I know you'll probably need

_____ a lot of shopping for your new home. Sam and I would really like _____ you a
    6   7

special present. Any ideas?

I think it's good that you decided _____ a small wedding. Small weddings are more personal.
                                        8

Well, I'm really looking forward to seeing you at the wedding.

Love,

Patricia

P.S.: Don't forget _____ me what you want for a present!
                        9

Answer these questions about yourself in complete sentences.

1. What do you like to do in your free time?

   _____

2. What do you know how to do well?

   _____

3. What do you plan to do this weekend?

   _____

4. What do you often forget to do?

   _____

5. What would you like to do after you finish studying English?

   _____

Lesson 2   It's an interesting idea.

Write two suggestions for each situation. Use comparative forms of the adjectives in the box.

exciting	disappointing	amusing	frustrating	entertaining	inspiring
charming	stimulating	boring	relaxing	challenging	embarrassing

Jodi is *frustrated* with her new pet.

1. <u>She should get a more exciting pet.</u>
   <u>She should look for a less frustrating pet.</u>

The Nguyens are *disappointed* in the movie.

2. _____

Heejung and Gita are *annoyed* with their friend Trish.

3. _____

Carmen is *bored* with her work.

4. _____

Read about two vacations. Then answer the questions in complete sentences with *because*.

Mountain Adventure Direct (MAD)

Spend four thrilling days and three inspiring nights as you explore the Colorado wilderness.

Our trained guides will take you over mountains and across rivers.
- Horseback riding
- White-water rafting
- Wilderness camping

Call 1-800-555-6285 for further information.

Gulf Cruises Unlimited

Travel in luxury aboard the newly renovated *Princess Marissa*. Three-, five-, and seven-day cruises available.

✳ Swimming Pools
✳ Luxury suites
✳ Four-star dining
✳ Live bands
✳ Excursions to tropical islands

Call 1-800-Marissa. One of our charming representatives will be happy to serve you.

1. Which vacation is more relaxing? Why?

   _____

2. Which vacation is more exciting? Why?

   _____

3. Which vacation is more interesting to you? Why?

   _____

Gulf Cruises asks passengers to fill out the following questionnaire at the end of their trip. Read one customer's response and correct his five errors. (The first one has been done for you.)

THANK YOU FOR TRAVELING ON THE *MARISSA*

We would like to hear about your experiences. Please take a few minutes to answer these questions.

What did you like? The service was ~~pleased~~ *pleasing*. The crew members were charming. I was very satisfying with their service. Also, the trips to the islands were excited.

Were you disappointed with your trip in any way? Please explain. I was dissatisfied with the food. We had to wait a long time to eat, and the food was bored and overcooked.

Other comments? Except for badly cooking food, I had a very relaxing voyage.

Read the conversation between Ms. Chin and an operator at a credit card agency. Circle the correct form of the word.

Operator: Hello. How may I help you?

Ms. Chin: Yes, your company has made an error on my credit card bill, and I am ___*annoyed / annoying*___ .
1

Operator: What is the problem?

Ms. Chin: I was overcharged for some airplane tickets. I bought two tickets, but I was charged for four tickets!

Operator: Oh, I guess the travel agent was ___*distracted / distracting*___ . They're very busy these
2
days.

Ms. Chin: That's no excuse. We were ___*embarrassed / embarrassing*___ because of the mistake. While
3
we were on our trip, my husband and I were ___*surprised / surprising*___ when our
4
credit card was declined in a restaurant. It was a ___*shocked / shocking*___
5
experience, and it was not our fault. We had not overspent our credit limit.

Operator: Oh, that's terrible. You must have felt very ___*frustrated / frustrating*___ . I'll contact
6
the airline and have the correction made immediately.

Exercise 5

Describe the scene in your own words. How does each person feel?

_____

_____

_____

_____

Lesson 3 Could you help me, please?

════════════════════ **Exercise 1** ════════════════════

Match each of these requests to one of the following situations.

> Could you please tell me the assignment again?
> Would you mind turning the TV down a little?
> Can you tell me where the post office is?
> Would you show me some of the features of this model?
> ✔ Would you push 4, please?
> Will you tell me when the light turns green?
> Could you please send an extra towel to Room 308?
> I'm late for my flight. Can you drive faster?

1. _Would you push 4, please?_____

2. _____

3. _____

4. _____

5. _____

6. _____

7. _____

8. _____

Exercise 2

You are a guest at the hotel. Make a polite request for each of these situations.

1. You want a map of the city.

_____

2. You have a lot of luggage. You want someone to carry it to your room for you.

_____

3. There is too much noise coming out of the room next door. You're talking to the front desk about it.

_____

4. You want to make a long-distance call from your room.

_____

5. You want the concierge to call you a taxi.

_____

6. You want to pay the hotel bill with a check instead of a credit card.

_____

A hotel receptionist is talking to a guest on the phone. Complete their conversation.

Guest:	Can you send someone over to change the sheets ?
	₁
Operator:	The sheets were changed this morning, ma'am. Would you like to have them changed again?
Guest:	No, that's OK. But ————————————?
	₂
Operator:	Sure. How many towels do you need?
Guest:	Two, please. And while you're at it, ————————?
	₃
Operator:	There are some hangers in the closet. Would you like some more?
Guest:	No, that's fine. I didn't know there were any. Oh, ———————— .
	₄
Operator:	Three extra pillows. Sure. Anything else?
Guest:	Oh, yes. ————————————.
	₅
	I have to have a hot water bottle to be able to sleep.
Operator:	I don't think we have any hot water bottles, ma'am.
Guest:	————————————?
	₆
Operator:	Send someone to the drugstore to get one? Sorry, but I don't think there's anybody who can do that for you.
Guest:	Gee, now I'm going to be awake the whole night.
Operator:	On second thought, I think I can go get it for you myself.

These two pictures look the same at first, but if you look closely, you will notice several differences. Describe the differences. Use the following words.

windows	hangers	dust
pictures	sunlight	furniture

Room 201 *Room 716*

1. <u>There is more furniture in Room 201 than in Room 716.</u>
2. _____
3. _____
4. _____
5. _____
6. _____

Exercise 5

Would you rather stay in Room 201 or Room 716? Using the sentences you wrote for Exercise 4, write a paragraph about the room you would prefer to stay in and why.

_____
_____
_____
_____
_____
_____
_____

UNIT 10

Lesson 1 Take the Thai cooking class.

=== Exercise 1 ===

Pia enjoys taking classes in her free time, and she has many hobbies. Look at the different courses that Pia has taken. Then match the sentence parts below to read her advice.

Pottery: Learn to make your own pots, cups, and vases.
Six-week course meets T/Th 7–9 P.M.
Materials fee: $50.
Messy but fun

Folk dancing: Traditional dances of Eastern Europe are introduced and practiced in this ongoing course.
Dance classes are held every Friday and Saturday night 7–9 P.M.
A lot of great people!

Flower arranging: Learn to make everything from bridal bouquets to festive holiday centerpieces.
One-month course meets every Saturday 9 A.M.–2 P.M.
Materials fee: $60.
Wear a sweater. Room is cold.

Acoustic guitar: Become familiar with basic guitar chords and learn to play simple songs. Two-month course meets T/Th from 7–9 P.M.
(Students must bring their own instruments.)
Remember to keep guitar in tune!

Thai cooking: Discover the flavors of Thailand as you learn to prepare classical Thai dishes such as Swimming Angel and Pad Thai. (One dinner will be prepared and eaten by participants at every session.)
Six-week course meets on Monday evenings 5–8:30 P.M.
Materials fee: $72.
Spicy and delicious

Papermaking: Make beautiful paper stationery or gift wrap using exotic ingredients such as onion skin and wildflowers.
Four-week course meets Wednesday evenings 7–9 P.M.
Materials fee: $35.
Wildflower paper is good for invitations.

1. ___C___ If you like to get your hands dirty,
2. _____ If you take flower arranging,
3. _____ If you want to make spicy, delicious meals,
4. _____ If you want to get a lot of exercise,
5. _____ If you take the guitar class,
6. _____ If you make your own paper,

a. take the Thai cooking class.
b. don't forget to tune your guitar.
c. take a pottery class.
d. you can use it for invitations.
e. take the folk-dancing class.
f. wear a sweater.

Pia and her co-worker Jae are taking guitar lessons this winter, but they have a few problems, and they are often late to class. Look at the following list of problems and add possible solutions to the sentences. Check the best solution for each problem.

- They both work in an office downtown.
- Guitar lessons are on the north side of town.
- Pia lives near class, but Jae's apartment is on the west side.
- They both want to eat dinner before class.
- They need to bring their guitars to class.
- They do not have cars.

Example

_____✓_____ If Jae leaves his guitar at Pia's apartment, _he does not have to go home to get it._

_____ If Jae and Pia bring their guitars to work, _they worry about where to keep them._

_____ If they eat dinner in a restaurant, _____

_____ If they eat dinner at Pia's house, _____

_____ If they eat dinner after class, _____

_____ If they walk to class, _____

_____ If they take a bus to class, _____

_____ If they try to ride their bicycles to class, _____

Read the following conversation between Jae and Pia. Add the four missing commas.

Jae: I get annoyed if I don't have time to practice the guitar. I hate making mistakes in class.

Pia: Really? If I made a fool out of myself I wouldn't care at all.

Jae: I guess I'm a perfectionist. If things don't go the way I plan I can't work.

Pia: We're different then. I get bored if I have to do things the same way twice.

Jae: I think it's a good thing that I'm in accounting and you're in marketing then!

Are you more like Jae or more like Pia? Read the following sentences and put a check mark next to the sentences that describe you.

_____   1. I get discouraged if I do not finish my work on time.
_____   2. I forget about time if I am interested in a project.
_____   3. I feel content if I have clear goals.
_____   4. I feel unhappy if I have to follow a lot of rules.
_____   5. I feel interested if I can try different methods when I am working.
_____   6. I like to finish one project completely before I start another.

Review your sentences and check the statement below that best describes you.

_____ I am an experimenter.   _____ I am a perfectionist.

Reread the sentences you marked in Exercise 4. Then write a paragraph explaining what kind of worker you are. Provide specific examples to support your opinion.

_____

_____

_____

_____

_____

_____

Lesson 2   You might have a good time.

════════════════════ **Exercise 1** ════════════════════

Complete the journal entries with *might, might not, could,* or *couldn't*.

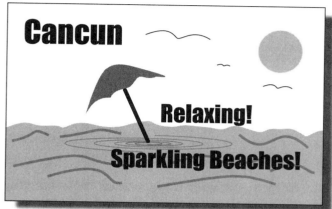

Tuesday, March 10

   I can't believe I'm finally taking a vacation! I've been looking forward to this for a long time, and I want to go someplace really special. I _____might_____ go to New York. The last
                                                           1
time I wanted to go, I _____ find a good price for plane tickets. Now, however, the
                                2
airlines _____ have more reasonable prices. Yes, New York _____ be fun.
              3   4
I'll call my travel agent. He _____ know of a special deal with hotel and airline
                                         5
tickets. I _____ even get tickets for a Broadway show or a basketball game.
               6

Wednesday, March 11

   Well, it looks as if New York _____ be such a good idea after all. Airline tickets
                                         7
are more expensive again, and all the decent hotels are booked. However, my travel agent
thinks I _____ enjoy going to the beach. He says I _____ spend ten days
              8   9
in Cancun for the price of seven days in New York. It _____ rain in the evenings,
                                                                 10
but the mornings and afternoons are usually sunny. On second thought, my Spanish isn't that
good—I _____ understand the people. I guess I _____ buy a good
              11   12
English/Spanish dictionary, though. Or better yet, Rosa _____ want to go with me.
                                                                      13
And her Spanish is perfect!

Complete the paragraph. Use *may* or *might* and the verbs provided.

People with a common cold (*experience*) __may experience__ one or more of the following
                                              1

symptoms. They (*feel*) _____ feverish or irritable; they (*have*) _____ a
                            2   3

runny nose or sore throat; or their arms and legs (*ache*) _____. However, if the
                                                               4

person has a sore throat with a fever and swollen glands, an earache, or deep cough, then that

person (*be*) _____ suffering from a bacterial infection and not just a common cold. If
                  5

that is the case, he or she (*need*) _____ to see a doctor as soon as possible.
                                          6

===== **Exercise 3** =====

**Martin has just spent two weeks in a physical fitness training camp. He made a check mark
next to the things he was able to do before camp and the things he is able to do now. Write
sentences about his progress using the correct form of *be able to*.**

	Before	Now
run five miles	X	✓
swim the length of the pool under water	X	✓
throw a javelin 100 feet	X	X
jump a hurdle on horseback	X	X
hit a bull's-eye with a bow and arrow	X	✓
paddle a canoe across the lake	✓	✓

1. Before camp, __Martin wasn't able to run five miles.__
   Now __he's able to run them.__
2. He __wasn't able to throw a javelin 100 feet before camp,__
   and he still __isn't able to throw it.__
3. He _____ before,
   and he _____ now, too.
4. He _____ before camp,
   and he still _____
5. Now he _____, but before camp
   _____
6. Before camp, he _____,
   but now he _____

Complete the conversation between Harry and his father. Use *can, can't, could, couldn't,* **or the appropriate form of** *be able to.*

Dad: *(fix)* _Were you able to fix_ the lawn mower, Harry?
               ⌞1⌟

Harry: No, so I *(mow)* _____ the lawn until tomorrow.
                                        2

Dad: *(help)* _____ you _____ me with the kitchen, then? I
                                                         3
               want to start painting it in a few minutes.

Harry: Gee, Dad, I have to clean the basement for Mom first.

Dad: Well, *(paint)* _____ you _____ later?
                                                              4

Harry: Yeah, I *(help)* _____ you after lunch.
                                      5

Dad: By the way, *(find)* _____ you _____ that tie you bor-
                                                                      6
               rowed last night?

Harry: Uh . . . no. I've looked everywhere, and I *(find)* _____ it. But I'll keep
                                                                                7
               looking.

Dad: It was my favorite tie!

Harry: I know, Dad. If I *(find)* _____ it, I'll buy you a new one.
                                                 8

Read the following passage. There are eight mistakes in the forms of *can* **and** *be able to.* **Find and correct them. (The first one has been done for you.)**

              couldn't
There were many things I ~~can't~~ do before I came to this school. For one thing, I couldn't not stand up in front of a class and give a speech. I remember the first time I had to describe my country. I wasn't able open my mouth. My hands started to sweat, and my legs began to shake. Finally, the teacher called on another student and I could to sit down.

Now I could take risks. I able to feel comfortable about doing something slightly unusual and possibly making a mistake. I can learn and enjoy the learning process at the same time. The informal atmosphere of my English class can to provide a supportive atmosphere and a safe place to become comfortable with the language before trying it out in the real world. I can finally seeing how my speaking skills have really improved in this "chatty" class.

Lesson **3**   I'll let you know.

Look at the pictures of Jae and his fiancée, Sima. Complete the sentences.

1. I'll marry Sima _after I find a good job._
   _____

2. We'll buy new furniture _____
   _____

3. If I buy a van, _____
   _____

4. As soon as we move into our new house,
   _____

Read Sima's e-mail message to her mother about her summer plans. Put in the five missing commas. (The first one has been done for you.)

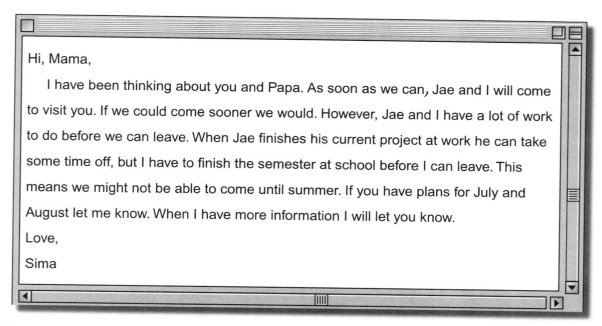

Hi, Mama,

    I have been thinking about you and Papa. As soon as we can, Jae and I will come to visit you. If we could come sooner we would. However, Jae and I have a lot of work to do before we can leave. When Jae finishes his current project at work he can take some time off, but I have to finish the semester at school before I can leave. This means we might not be able to come until summer. If you have plans for July and August let me know. When I have more information I will let you know.

Love,

Sima

Read the response that Sima's mother wrote. Find and correct the five tense errors. (The first one has been done for you.)

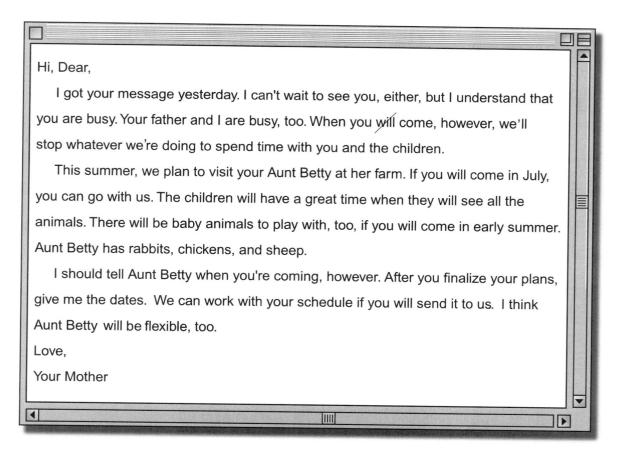

Hi, Dear,

    I got your message yesterday. I can't wait to see you, either, but I understand that you are busy. Your father and I are busy, too. When you will come, however, we'll stop whatever we're doing to spend time with you and the children.

    This summer, we plan to visit your Aunt Betty at her farm. If you will come in July, you can go with us. The children will have a great time when they will see all the animals. There will be baby animals to play with, too, if you will come in early summer. Aunt Betty has rabbits, chickens, and sheep.

    I should tell Aunt Betty when you're coming, however. After you finalize your plans, give me the dates. We can work with your schedule if you will send it to us. I think Aunt Betty will be flexible, too.

Love,

Your Mother

Read the speech that Jae's boss, Mr. Anderson, gave to his sales staff. Then read the statements below. Make a check mark next to the statements that accurately represent Mr. Anderson's meaning.

Greetings, Friends and Colleagues,

Thank you for coming today. I'm sure a lot of you would rather be digging ditches in the hot sun than listening to me talk, but I've got some good news for you, so I hope you'll stay and listen for a few minutes while I talk about developments in our company's new line of cars.

We have spent the past few months improving the air-conditioning system in next year's GTX sedan, and I'm happy to say that it is powerful. If you wanted to, you could probably make ice cubes in the ashtray. And not only is the A/C powerful, but the heat works pretty well too! Turn that heater on and you could melt snow ten feet away. This car is equipped for all kinds of weather.

Another improvement concerns the brake system. We've always had a good reputation for speed, but people care about brakes too, and so far tests indicate that the GTX performs better than last year's model. Front air bags on both the driver and passenger sides are another new safety feature. For families with children, we have optional child safety car seats that buckle into the back seat of the vehicle.

Finally, this car is glamorous. We've redesigned the exterior to appeal to customers who want a classy look for a low price. You single people won't stay single for long if you drive this car. I guarantee it!

All this is to say, this is a great car, and I believe you people are going to have an easy year. This beautiful little baby is going to sell itself.

_____ 1. The purpose of Mr. Anderson's speech is to motivate salespeople to sell the new model GTX sedan.

_____ 2. When Mr. Anderson suggests that people would rather be digging ditches, he is trying to be funny.

_____ 3. People will be able to make ice cubes in the GTX sedan's ashtray.

_____ 4. The new model GTX sedan is faster than the previous one.

_____ 5. Mr. Anderson believes that people who drive a nice car are more popular with the opposite sex.

_____ 6. Mr. Anderson doesn't think he needs salespeople to sell the GTX sedan.